A WITNESS FOR

Him

DIANE YODER

A WITNESS FOR *Him*

Minerva finds peace despite the ravages of polio

ISBN: 978-1-941213-77-3

Cover photo: © www.shutterstock.com
Cover and layout design: Lydia Zook

Printed in the USA

For more information about Christian Aid Ministries,
see page 187.

Published by:
TGS International
P.O. Box 355
Berlin, Ohio 44610 USA
Phone: 330-893-4828
Fax: 330-893-2305
www.tgsinternational.com

TGS001071

Dedication

To Minerva and Lovina,
whose lives have blessed countless people.
This book was written with love.

Table of Contents

Acknowledgements ... ix

1. The Farm Girl ... 1
2. Family and School ... 11
3. Epidemic ... 23
4. Hospital Time ... 31
5. Wedding Cake Therapy ... 37
6. Experiments ... 45
7. Giving Thanks ... 55
8. Adjustments ... 61
9. Step by Step ... 67
10. Where Is Home? ... 75
11. In Search of Sleep ... 85
12. Milestones ... 91
13. The Family Grows ... 99
14. Adventures with the Youth Group ... 107
15. Aunt Nervie and Aunt Vina ... 115
16. A Full Life ... 121
17. Dad ... 127
18. Travels ... 135
19. Tracheotomy ... 141
20. Burdens ... 147
21. Sorrow ... 153
22. A Passing ... 159
23. Surgery ... 165
24. Celebrations ... 173
    Afterword ... 181
    A Note from the Author ... 183
    About the Author ... 185

Acknowledgements

WITH APPRECIATION TO . . .

- Minerva and Lovina Gingerich, for sharing your story with me. I very much enjoyed getting to know you. May God bless you richly as you continue to be shining lights for Him!

- Ida Friesen, for your willingness to show me the places where Minerva spent time as a child.

- All those in Plain City, Ohio, who took an interest in the writing of this book and encouraged me in it.

- My friends and family, who covered me with intercessory prayer while I worked on this project.

- Most of all, I praise God for His guiding hand in this venture. May He receive all the glory.

On a nice winter day in 1938
Minerva was born, December 7 the date;
Look! What a pretty baby—black hair and dark eyes;
She was the joy of the family, we will surmise.

When she began to toddle, she was such a sight;
From morning till noon, and on into the night,
In the cupboards, in the drawers, and into the sink—
What she didn't get into was hard to think.

And then she grew older, a pretty little miss,
But one day something happened—just listen to this,
Her mother noticed she wasn't feeling well,
And soon was quite sick—it wasn't hard to tell.

To the doctor—to the hospital—oh no!
"Please, Lord, let her live! We all love her so!"
She was smitten with the dreaded disease: polio,
And became paralyzed—but her smile could still go.

For many months we waited and prayed,
And Minerva came home—but in the iron lung lay;
What a joy to have her home, her voice to hear;
All who visited heard nothing but cheer.

What happy years to follow, with the young folks she went
To cottage meetings, rest homes, or wherever she was sent,
Bringing smiles and cheer to downhearted souls,
Serving her Lord—this was her utmost goal.

From the depths of our hearts, we thank Minerva, our friend,
For the joy and happiness to us she has sent;
We pray God will be with her till He calls her home,
And her body is made perfect, gathered 'round His Throne.[1]

---

[1] This poem was written by Esther (Kurtz) Troyer, 2-5-80.

CHAPTER ONE

The Farm Girl

Autumn 1946
Plain City, Ohio

An early frost glittered on the ground. Minerva hurried through the gate into the pasture, shivering as the cool air touched her face. Mom wasn't very strict about wearing shoes in cool weather, and Minerva liked to go barefoot as long as she could. Picking up a stick, she broke into a run.

Tall grasses waved about her, still lush and green in the late summer. The chill in the air painted a flush of color in Minerva's narrow face. She was eight now, active and carefree. She much preferred to play outside than curl up on a cozy chair and read a book.

The herd of cows was only a short distance away. There were twenty-one in all, some grazing and others lying in the grass. Waving her stick, Minerva ran toward them. When the closest cow lumbered to her feet, Minerva quickly stepped into the area she'd just vacated and warmed her feet. The sun was peeking over the trees now, but it would be awhile before the ground responded to its warmth.

As she followed the cows out of the pasture toward the barn, Minerva joined the birds' chorus with her own song. Dad always led out in family devotions right after breakfast, and she felt that reading the Bible and praying to God brightened her whole day. The melody she was singing now was one she'd learned the night before, when Dad had lined up his family after supper and taught them a new song. They often sang together in the evenings.

Minerva stopped singing when she came into the barnyard. Who was talking with Dad up by the chicken house? The man turned, and his dark eyes began to twinkle in her direction. Minerva grinned back and went on to the barn without slowing down. Alphonso Cincioni, the Italian music director from Plain City Elementary, was here to buy eggs. Many people came to buy eggs from them. No doubt he thought it was funny to see her barefoot, but Minerva didn't care. She was a farm girl!

Mom and Verna were both in the barn getting ready to milk the cows when Minerva came inside. Minerva stood close to Mom as she pulled up a stool and sat down beside Becky. "Someday we'll let you milk this cow, Minerva," Mom said with a smile. "She has such short teats that it's hard to milk her. With your short fingers, you'll be able to milk her better than the rest of us."

Holding out her hands, Minerva studied them. Yes, they were small, just like Mom had said. She had never thought of it before. "I can't wait until Dad lets me milk," she said.

"Your day is coming," Verna spoke up. She was sitting on a stool beside another cow, the bucket already half filled with milk. At thirteen, Verna was a good worker. "Dad says that he isn't going to get milkers until all his children learn to milk by hand."

Most of Minerva's nine siblings were battling the measles at this time. Both Verna and Minerva had recovered from it earlier. Now Minerva glanced out the open door. Dad was coming to the barn, and Alphonso Cincioni's car was just pulling out of the driveway behind him. Turning, she raced toward her dad. "Will you teach me how to milk this morning?"

Jonas grinned down at his daughter. "My, you're ambitious, aren't you? Perhaps I'll teach you when I have more time. I'm rather in a hurry today. After we're finished with the chores, I'd like to go to town."

"Oh, take me with you! Please?" She didn't get to go to town very often.

"Well, let's first see what your mother says." Jonas led her into the barn and stopped beside his wife. "Minerva would like to go with me this morning, Emma. What do you think? I'm going to ask the community people if they are willing to give money to help build our school."

"That's fine with me. But stay close to Dad, Minerva," Emma warned. "We don't want you getting lost. Change into a good dress before you go, and get your shawl. And put shoes on your feet!"

Minerva grinned at that and ran out the door. Behind her, she heard Dad chuckle and call out, "Slow down, Minnie. It'll be a while yet before we go."

And indeed it was. Minerva was ready ten minutes before Dad finally pulled up to the yard gate with the horse and buggy. Hurrying out, she climbed onto the seat next to her father. She normally sat in the back with the rest of her siblings when the whole family was along, but not today.

Dad was driving Betty, one of his fast horses. Sometimes when Dad told Minerva to run an errand for him, he'd say, "Run fast like Betty!" He had owned the horse since before he was married. Dad had another horse that Minerva liked a lot. Bonnie was tame and didn't act up like Betty sometimes did.

Minerva glanced around, taking in a deep breath of the tangy air. The sky was deep blue with fleecy white clouds, and the sun shone brightly. "It's beautiful today, isn't it?" she asked aloud. "I can't wait until we have the new school," she chattered on without waiting for an answer. "I don't mind public school, but I'm ready for our own!" She knew that Dad was one of those helping to start their church school. Because of the influences at public school, the Amish and Mennonites wanted to start their own.

But for now, she was going to public school. She liked it even though she didn't always get the best grades. She always found arithmetic and spelling hard work. With her outgoing nature, she quickly made friends among the other children. She never minded when they gave her their money and asked her to buy ice cream cones for them on the second floor. It was a treat go to up there, even though she never bought ice cream there for herself.

This year, Minerva had also attended a summer Bible school at Sharon Mennonite Church. Many children attended every summer, going in the forenoon every day for a week to learn about God and His Word. The teachers taught new songs and interesting Bible lessons. Minerva always felt excited when it was time for summer Bible school.

Dad was stopping the horse at a hitching post next to the hardware store. He jumped down from the buggy and turned to help Minerva. She waited while he tied the horse to the post, and then she followed him inside.

"Howdy, Jonas!" Dewitt Norris, the clerk, greeted her dad as they entered. Here in Plain City, Ohio, everyone knew each other. Dad returned his greeting and went on down the aisle, his boots clomping against the floor. Its wooden planks were kept clean with linseed oil.

Minerva followed close behind, her dark eyes taking in every-thing. She wished Ida could be here with her. Though Ida was four years younger than she, they did everything together. But now her sister was at home, lying sick in bed. Minerva couldn't wait for the day when her whole family would be well again.

Two weeks passed, and the family was up and about again. Minerva worked beside her younger brother Lester in the loafing barn, using a hay fork to scatter straw across the floor for the cows. During autumn and winter, they always bedded down here for the night.

Bits of straw clung to Minerva's arms as she paused to rest. She brushed a dark strand of hair from her face and looked over at Lester. "Will we be done soon?" she asked impatiently. "I wanted to play in the woodshed."

Lester glanced up. "Go put some straw over there." He pointed toward the left corner and turned back to his own work. Minerva sighed and started toward the corner he'd indicated. She didn't see the hay fork protruding out of the straw until it was too late.

"Oww!" she screamed as the tine sank into her foot. Lester bounded toward her across the straw, his face white. "Help me to the house," she whispered, holding her foot. Blood trickled through her fingers, and she tried to hold back her tears as Lester helped her to her feet.

"Can you stand? Here, lean on me." He walked slowly, leading the way out of the barn. Minerva hopped along beside him, grateful for his help.

As Lester led the way into the kitchen, their mother hurried toward them. "What happened? Here, sit down in a chair," she instructed without waiting for an answer. "We'll soak your foot in water with disinfectant, and then I'll get a bandage for it."

"We were forking straw in the loafing barn," Lester explained.

"A hay fork was buried in the hay, and one of the tines got in her foot."

Minerva bit her lip against the pain as Mom carefully lowered her foot into the bucket of water. Ida came running over to watch, her small, round face worried. "Does it hurt badly, Minerva?"

Minerva smiled bravely. "Mom's taking good care of me."

"It will probably heal again before long," Mom said, carefully wrapping the bandage around Minerva's foot. "But you won't be able to do much until then."

Minerva sat on a chair at the kitchen table, watching her mom and older sisters bustle around the kitchen as they made supper. The salmon soup smelled so good, and Mom set out crackers to go with it. At last the others came in from doing chores, and her sisters hurried to fill the glasses on the table with water.

Her two big brothers, Ora and Noah, were the first to come into the kitchen. "What's going on here?" Noah asked, stopping beside her. "Did you hurt your foot?"

"Can't you see that I did?" she responded, lifting the bandaged foot for him to see. "I was forking straw and stepped on a hay fork."

"I'm sorry you got hurt," he said, and she could see in his eyes that he meant it.

The others were coming in now, gathering around the table. Mom and Dad sat down at one end, with Ida between them. Ora sat at the other end, with Noah beside him. Lovina was on Ora's right, with Fannie and Verna. Dan, Andy, Lester, and Minerva filled the long bench against the wall.

After prayer, the boys peppered Minerva with questions. Each of them had his own idea of what she should have done while forking straw, and what she should do now. Finally, Dad looked over and said, "Not so noisy, children." He often said that when he was trying to talk with someone else and they got too loud. Minerva couldn't imagine it being quiet at mealtime—not with twelve people around the table.

The girls always took turns after supper washing the dishes while the rest went to the living room. Ora helped Minerva to the couch, where Dad was already lining up the children along the wall from the oldest to youngest. "I want to teach you a song tonight," he said. "It's called 'No Tears in Heaven.' I think it'll be fairly easy to learn."

As their father began to sing, the beauty of the words struck Minerva. "No tears in heaven, no sorrows given, all will be glory in that land; There'll be no sadness, all will be gladness, when we shall join that happy band . . ."[1]

She sat still, deep in thought. *No tears in heaven?* She listened closely as Dad sang the chorus. "No tears in heaven fair, no tears, no tears up there; sorrow and pain will all have flown . . . no tears in heaven will be known."

She joined in as her siblings began to sing. This was a song she would always remember.

Minerva turned nine in December. Six inches of snow blanketed the ground, and she could no longer go barefoot outside. Instead, she donned her thickest coat and hood. She loved going outdoors with her brothers and sisters to build snowmen, make snow angels, and play Fox-and-Geese. It always felt so good to come inside again and stand by the wood stove to warm up.

That was the month their new church school opened its doors to students for the first time. It was built with brick and had four rooms—two downstairs and two upstairs. But only

[1] Fanny Crosby, 1868. Public domain.

Lovina and Fannie were able to attend now. Even though the school wasn't completely ready yet, the school board wanted to give high schoolers a chance to attend a Christian school before they graduated. There would be room for more lower graders to start attending the next fall.

On Christmas morning, Minerva awakened before the rest of the house was stirring. She slid out of bed, shivering in the frigid air, and dressed quickly in the pretty blue dress Mom had finished sewing for her just the week before. Then she skipped downstairs to the living room where she could warm up by the wood stove.

Dad and Mom were already there, sitting together near the wood stove in the calm stillness of the morning. As Minerva entered, Emma turned and smiled at her daughter. "You're already awake, Minnie-mine?"

Minerva smiled back and came to stand beside her, holding out her hands to the warmth of the fire. "I woke up early."

"Too excited to sleep?" Dad asked teasingly.

She grinned at him, visions of candy beginning to dance through her mind. Dad always brought candy home at Christmas, and he allowed them to eat more than usual. "Where is the candy?" she asked eagerly, bouncing on her tiptoes. "Is it on the library table again like usual?"

He laughed and reached out to tousle her black hair. "Why don't you go look?"

She didn't need a second invitation. Running into the next room, she saw it first thing—a mouth-watering display of chocolate drops and chocolate-covered peanut clusters, all piled together in a dish. This year Dad had even bought hardtack ribbon candy. Hardtack was syrup cooked until it was hard and brittle, then cut into little strips and pieces. Minerva's favorite, though, were the chocolate-covered peanuts. She took one from the dish and popped it into her mouth.

Dad came into the room behind her. "Here's something else I brought home." He placed a long Hershey bar on the library table and set a knife beside it. "You can chip away whatever you want to eat off of it with this knife."

By now the others were coming downstairs, eager to see what candy Dad had brought home this year. Minerva stayed for a little while before wandering toward the kitchen, where Mom and the older girls were cooking breakfast. She peeked into the pot Verna was stirring on the stove. The oatmeal smelled delicious!

As they gathered around the table to eat, Minerva felt so happy it seemed that her heart would burst. Her family was a treasure.

CHAPTER TWO

Family and School

Summer 1949

Sunlight streamed through the car windows, touching Minerva's face with warmth. She shifted uncomfortably in her seat. Though the Hudson car was long and wide, it seemed tight with eleven people inside.

"We'll be stopping to eat soon," Dad said, glancing back at her from the passenger's seat. Minerva shifted again, this time with excitement. She could hardly wait to get out and run!

"Let's play tag when we get out," Wilma said from beside her. All six girls were packed into the back seat—Minerva, Ida, and Verna, along with their cousins, Wilma, Esther, and Erma. Their parents rode up front. Perry and Fannie Stutzman had asked Dad and Mom to travel with them up to Canada for a two-week trip. They had seen much beautiful scenery, like Mackinac Island's four great lakes. But now they were heading home, with plans to see Niagara Falls in New York. First, though, they had to get supper somewhere and travel to a cabin for the night.

They stopped at a restaurant in town. There was a picnic area next to it with a welcoming lawn. As soon as their driver parked the Hudson, the doors flew open and all six girls tumbled out. How good it felt to run after sitting so long!

Minutes later Mom called them for supper. The ladies had

spread it out on a picnic table, and Minerva came close to look it over. Along with toasted cheese sandwiches, there were also glasses filled with a frosty drink that she had never seen before.

"Those milkshakes look good, don't they?" Aunt Fannie asked with a smile.

Milkshakes! Though she'd never had one, Minerva knew they were made from ice cream and milk. Her dark eyes sparkled back at Aunt Fannie. "Can I taste a little before supper?"

Mom laughed. "I think you can wait until after we pray."

Minerva glanced toward Dad and Uncle Perry, visiting together as they sauntered slowly toward them. She wished they would hurry. She could hardly wait to drink that milkshake.

It was just as good as she thought it would be, thick and white and creamy. She drank slowly, savoring every sip. The cold drink was delicious on this July evening.

After supper was over, they drove on to their cabin nestled in the mountains. The girls helped the adults unload the Hudson and then went outside to chase fireflies. Their lights flickered here, then there, as darkness slowly deepened around them. At last Minerva sank down onto the cabin's porch beside Dad, tired but happy. She held a firefly on her finger, watching its light flicker on and off.

"We should make it to Niagara Falls by mid-morning," Dad was saying. He glanced down at her and rested his hand on her head. "So get your rest tonight, Minnie. There's going to be a lot of walking tomorrow."

She grinned up at him and felt that she couldn't wait for the next day.

Great torrents of water rushed in a thundering roar over the cliff, falling to the rocks below. Minerva stood watching the majestic sight, strands of hair flying in the wind. She leaned close to Verna. "Isn't it amazing?"

Verna nodded, her eyes wide with wonder. "Niagara Falls makes a person feel so small."

Dad turned and smiled at them. "It's God's handiwork. I think this is something the rest of our family needs to see too," he added to Mom. "Maybe they could come up here before the school year starts."

At the thought of her brothers and sisters back home, Minerva's heart gave an excited little jump. She could hardly wait to see all of them again.

When Dad said he might do something, he was likely to carry it out. A month later he took the rest of the family to see Niagara Falls in New York. Only Ora stayed behind to do chores and keep company with those who had already visited the falls. Although the travelers couldn't stay long because of school starting shortly, they had a successful sightseeing trip.

This was the second year Minerva would attend their church school. "I'm ready for fifth grade now," she said one evening. "I can hardly wait until school starts!"

It was after supper on a Saturday night, and they were all in the living room. The house was spotless, because they planned to host church the next day. The Amish gathered at the Gingerich house every Sunday during one summer month—twice for church, with Sunday school in between. Minerva's aunts had come over to help clean that morning. They had washed all the windows in the house and had polished pots and pans with SOS pads until they shone. Benches were set up in the house and on the porch for seating.

Now Minerva sat on the couch beside her mom, watching her mend socks. Wherever there was a hole, Mom would put the sock over a light bulb and stitch around a patch over the hole. She paused in her work to smile at Minerva. "My little girl is growing up!"

Minerva grinned back. For a moment she watched Mom's needle flash in and out through the sock. "Tell me about when you were a little girl, Mom," she said suddenly.

Emma laughed. "Haven't I told you before?"

"But I want to hear it again!" She sat up straighter. "What did you do when you were my age?"

Emma's needle slowed, and a thoughtful look came into her eyes. "I had to work hard when I was a girl, Minerva. Your grandmother was not a strong, healthy person. I had two older sisters, and we did most of the work."

Minerva couldn't imagine that. Her own mother was always busy—cooking, baking, cleaning, washing laundry, and doing sundry other tasks around the house. She was never idle.

"One of my sisters' names was Lovina," Mom said. "She got the flu and died when she was nineteen. Many people died from the flu that year."

Lovina glanced up. "I've always wished I could have met her."

"I had a lot of good times at home with my family, but there were some difficult times as well." Mom paused, that faraway look still in her eyes. "When Dad and I were planning to get married, my mom became so ill that we couldn't invite everyone we'd planned to. We had to cancel some of the invitations. But after the wedding she soon felt better."

"If there ever was a godly person, it was Grandma," Dad said. "She came from a spiritually strong family. Her father, Daniel E. Mast, was a deacon in the Amish church. He wrote articles for the *Herold der Wahrheit*.[1] It was a periodical for our people."

"He started it, didn't he?" Andy asked. He was sprawled on the floor, playing checkers with Dan.

"He was a promoter for it," Dad explained. "He was deeply concerned about the Amish church. He felt that some people were just living aimlessly and loosely. He had articles ready to go into the first issue. He wrote on many subjects, helping his readers live for God."

"Grandpa especially taught that salvation comes alone by faith," Mom added softly. "And he was a praying man."

Dad looked around at them all. "Children, you have godly generations behind you. Never take it for granted."

Minerva wished she could have met her great-grandfather, but he had died the day before her brother Dan was born. She turned to Dad. "Tell us about when you were a little boy."

Dad grinned at her and tweaked her nose. "You already know my story, just like you know Mom's."

"Tell it again!" Her dark eyes gleamed mischievously, and Dad chuckled.

"You know all too well that we'll tell our stories as often as you want us to." He sobered a little. "My mother died from cancer when I was seven, and Dad died from a heart attack when I was fourteen. They were older parents, since it was a second marriage for both of them. So that left all of us orphans—my younger brothers and me. After the funeral I went home with my half-brother, Jake Gingerich, who lived in Indiana. My brothers were placed in other homes. I came back here again when I was old enough and hired myself out to various people."

"Then you got married to Mom!" Ida exclaimed, and they all laughed.

"We were married on January 20, 1927," Dad said to Ida.

[1] This German word "Wahrheit" means "Truth."

Then he stopped, and the room grew quiet. Andy and Dan paused in their game of checkers to watch Dad. At length he said quietly, "I want to enjoy my family. I want to sing together and have family devotions. Most of all, I want my children to know and understand the Bible. I would have no greater joy than to know that all of you have given your hearts to the Lord and are walking with Him."

"You're like Great-Grandpa Mast," Minerva said softly.

There was a catch in Dad's voice when he answered. "I deeply appreciate your great-grandfather's example. He was a good man, and I want to stand for the same beliefs he taught."

Summer 1950

Minerva and Ida stood by the corral, watching Noah train his horse. Dixie was spirited and always gave their brother trouble whenever he drove her. Minerva could clearly remember the evening when she and Ida had gone with Mom and Dad to calling hours before a funeral. Their parents had planned to stay longer since Dad was taking care of the casket, so the girls wanted to go home with Noah, who had come over to chore for the bereaved family. However, Dixie wouldn't hold still long enough for the girls to get into the buggy. With Noah hanging on to the reins, she galloped toward the road and came back around the house, stopping at a different place from where the girls waited. So Noah drove around in a circle again, this time heading Dixie straight to them. They both quickly jumped on and were gone like the wind. Although the experience was frightening, they had arrived home safely.

Minerva jerked back to the present as the mare threw herself to the ground in the corral, her eyes rolling wildly. Ida jumped back. "Come on, let's go somewhere else! I don't want to watch anymore."

Minerva was glad to run after her sister to the house. Their dolls were patiently waiting on the porch where they had left them—one in a little crib made of wood, the other in a cradle made from orange crates. Minerva used the cradle. The cradle's ends were thick and heavy, and it had rockers on the bottom so she could rock it. Mom had sawed it by hand and painted it white, and Noah had made the wooden crib for Ida for her sixth birthday. With a glowing varnish, it was strong and beautiful.

"I wish Dad and Mom would get me a doll with hair," Ida said, picking up her doll from its crib. Minerva looked down at her own. Both dolls were small, with eyes that did not open and close.

"Well, at least we have beds for them," she said lightly. Wrapping her doll in a soft blanket, she laid it into the cradle and rocked it gently back and forth. "You know what? I'm going to name my baby Celesta."

Ida glanced up. "You mean after Noah and Lovina's baby girl?"

"That's right." They were neighbors, Noah Beachy owning a farm next to theirs. "She's such a cute little baby!"

Ida smiled. "Then I'll name my baby Leah," she declared. Leah was a cousin to baby Celesta, and had been born a dwarf. "She looks exactly like the real Leah, too, with light hair."

"Well, as long as our dolls don't have real hair, we can make them have whatever color hair we want!" Minerva laughed and jumped up. "I'm going to bake some pies for dinner."

Ida's eyes lit up. "I'll go with you."

The sidewalk between the house and woodshed was their own "kitchen," where they made pies out of mud, eggs, and elderberry flowers. But first they had to gather their ingredients. The elderberry bush grew beside the chicken house, and they hurried there first. Lester came up behind them as they filled their hands with the white clusters of dainty little flowers. "What are you doing?"

"We're making mud pies," Ida informed him. She plucked one last cluster of flowers from the bush. "Now we just need some eggs and mud."

"I found a sparrow's nest in the chicken house with eggs in it. I'll go get some." Lester was gone in a flash, and the girls went back to the sidewalk. By the time he returned with the little eggs, the girls had already mixed the elderberry flowers with mud. Carefully they cracked the eggs into the mixture and stirred until they dissolved. Last of all, they put the round mud pies on little flat canning lids to bake.

Minerva was just setting her mud pie on the chicken house roof to bake in the sun when she heard a sound that made her stand up straight. "Mrs. Norris's car is coming," she cried. The pie was forgotten as she quickly washed her hands at the pump and started running toward the road.

"Lovina's home!" Ida shouted, her own pie falling unheeded into the grass as she hurried after Minerva. Lester joined them in a race that ended near the road.

Lovina was coming up the walk toward the house, suitcase in hand, her dark hair shining in the sun. She was eighteen now, and she worked in town at Dewitt Norris's home. It was always a highlight for the children when she came home on weekends. As they reached her, she laughed. "I can always depend on you three to meet me whenever I come home!"

"I'll carry your suitcase," Lester said importantly.

"No, I will!" exclaimed Ida, reaching for the handle at the same time.

Lovina laughed again. "Such willing helpers! Why don't you let Lester carry it this time, Ida. I'll let you carry it the next time I come home. What were you in the middle of doing?"

All three talked at once, their words a jumble of dolls and mud pies and sparrow's nests. Mom was standing in the doorway, laughing, when they reached the porch. "Give Lovina a chance to talk, children! It's good to see you again," she added to Lovina, giving her a hug.

"Oh, you made pumpkin pie for supper!" exclaimed Lovina, stepping inside. "That looks so good. In town if I want pie, I have to bake it myself. They're never as good as yours."

Ida and Minerva grinned at each other. It was fun to bake their little mud pies, but when all was said and done, they'd much rather learn someday to bake like Mom and Lovina and make real pies.

Winter came again, and Minerva's brother Ora traveled to Florida for a vacation. One day the mail brought two packages, one for Minerva and one for Ida.

"They're from Ora," Mom told them, smiling. Minerva's hands trembled with excitement as she opened hers.

"Ohh," she breathed. "It's a pin cushion!" She held it up and turned it this way and that. The cushion was a soft shade of yellow, with a picture of a palm tree on one side. It was beautiful! She could imagine the twinkle in Ora's eyes when he'd purchased this tiny pin cushion for his little sister. "I'm going to tell him what a wonderful big brother he is when he comes home," she declared.

Mom laughed. "He's coming home next week for Noah's wedding. Why don't you tell him then?"

"I guess I could," Minerva agreed, her eyes lighting up. It was exciting to think about the wedding. Lots of company would be coming, and Mom had cleaned all week, polishing the house until it shone. Though she knew her brother would move away after the wedding, Minerva liked Noah's bride-to-be. Fannie was always kind. She and Noah always laughed about the time he'd been coming home from a visit with her and got stuck in the snow.

"I unhitched the horse and left the buggy there all night while I went to the neighbors to sleep," Noah would say, shaking his head. "I hope that doesn't happen again!"

Ora also had a special friend—a girl with the same name as his sister, Verna. She sometimes came over to spend time with their family, and once she had told the younger children, "When your brothers were teaching the youth how to sing 'No Tears in Heaven,' it was so quiet you could have heard a pin drop." Her voice was hushed, as though the memory still moved her. "We all liked that song."

The day of Noah's wedding dawned bright and cold. Since it was nine miles from their house, Dad had asked someone to take them with a car. Minerva thought Fannie looked so pretty in her pale blue dress. Noah was all spruced up and handsome, and his eyes shone whenever he looked at his bride. As Minerva watched them, she let herself daydream a little. It was exciting to think that she would have little nieces and nephews someday, like her cousin Katie. She wondered what her life would be like when she grew up.

She forgot about it, though, as she played with her cousins. Life was too interesting now to think of what might happen in the future. That was a long, long time away.

Laughter sounded across the playground as students spilled from the big yellow bus. They had made the bus ring with their songs, and now everyone was in good spirits as they hurried to the schoolhouse. Teacher Virginia Weaver stood watching at the window, a smile playing around her lips as she caught sight of one bright-eyed girl among the others. Minerva Gingerich was one of the most active girls she knew, a ray of sunshine. She never lacked friends, because she was jolly and friendly to all.

The students were coming up the steps now. The classroom for the fifth, sixth, and seventh graders was upstairs in the room toward the road. Virginia glanced across the thirty desks arranged in six rows. There was no electricity, but tall windows gave lots of light to see. She turned to the door as the first student entered and smiled. "Good morning!"

One by one the students passed her, returning her greeting as they went to their desks. Minerva was the last to enter, skipping into the room with her happy face glowing. "Hi!" She waved to Virginia as she plopped into her seat in the side row. Virginia smiled and turned to close the door. Another school day had begun.

The weather that day was nice enough to play softball. The girls raced each other to the ball field, all striving to catch up with the small girl in the lead. Minerva, glancing back, failed to see the dip in the ground before her. In an instant she had sprawled headlong to the ground. As the other girls sailed over her, she lay there giggling.

"Minerva!" One of the girls ran back to her. "Are you all right?"

"I'm fine!" Still laughing, Minerva jumped up. "Come on, let's go play ball!"

The noon hour seemed to fly by. Small and not as strong as some of the others, Minerva couldn't hit the ball very hard. But she cheered on her friends, enjoying the game to the fullest.

The summer school days faded slowly into autumn, and the wind tore red, orange, and yellow leaves from the trees. Then the weather turned colder, bringing snow and icicles that hung low from house roofs. Christmastime was one of Minerva's favorite seasons of the school year. The teachers and students drew names and gave each other gifts, and there was always the Christmas program to anticipate.

Every student had a part to memorize for the Christmas program, which was given on a homemade stage in one of the rooms upstairs. The teachers spent time decorating the room with fine artwork on the walls and flickering candles in evergreen wreaths. They hung lanterns on hooks from the ceiling and lit them.

This year Mom had sewn a new dress for Minerva—a deep green color that made her black hair look darker. The girl in the mirror that night had sparkling, dark eyes and a wide smile. And she sang her heart out with the rest of the chorus on stage.

Those in the audience watching could not know the future of that one slight girl on the stage, so vibrant and full of life. But God, all-knowing and all-wise, was watching her. "She is my precious daughter. I have plans for her . . ."

CHAPTER THREE

Epidemic
Summer 1952

"It's getting to be widespread," the lady said.

Minerva peeked around the corner. She didn't know what this lady's name was, but she recognized her from when she'd come earlier to buy eggs. The lady stood with Dad outside the door of the chicken house. "The polio epidemic is sweeping across the country," she went on. "Already there are many patients in the hospital."

"It's uncommon for the USA to suffer polio epidemics," Dad said, his brow furrowing.

"This year might be worse than it ever was before," the lady stated.

As she turned to leave, Minerva sprang back. Quickly she ran toward Ida, who was waiting for her at the end of the walk. "What were you doing?" Ida asked curiously.

"That lady who was just here said that a polio epidemic is sweeping across the country." Minerva pushed stray strands of black hair from her face. "She said lots of people are in the hospital with it."

Polio was a deadly disease. It first struck people with flu-like symptoms, but steadily worsened. If people survived it, they often became paralyzed, and the doctors had no cure for it.

But on this hot July day, polio seemed far away. "If it comes sweeping over us, we'll just duck!" Ida laughed and changed the subject. "Come on, let's go back to the fields. Mom said we can go with the men this morning while they bale hay."

Minerva's eyes lit up. The hay wagon was already waiting near the field. She and Ida quickly found a place to stand on the wagon with their brothers. As soon as Dad climbed into the tractor, they were off.

As they jolted along, the vibration seemed to go all through Minerva's body. That was unusual; normally she didn't mind the vibrations at all. But this time she stood on her tiptoes to ease her discomfort. In a few minutes it would probably go away.

"Here, Minerva. Swallow this pill, and soon you'll feel better."

Minerva groaned and opened her eyes. Mom stood next to her bed, feeling her forehead. She handed the small pill and a cup of water to Minerva. "I think it's just the flu, but it's going to keep you down for a few days."

Minerva managed to sit up. With shaking hands, she lifted the cup to her lips and took a sip of water to swallow the pill. Then she lay back again, exhausted. "I have the flu?"

"I think so. Ida got it during the night too. She threw up a few times just like you did." Mom turned to leave the room. "I'll be back soon with a piece of toast. That usually helps an upset stomach."

Minerva closed her eyes again. Only yesterday afternoon she'd been out on the wagon with Dad and the boys while they baled hay. She hadn't been feeling completely well, but now she was definitely sick.

As the days passed by, Minerva grew even more ill. Ida, too, still needed care. Mom, their faithful caretaker, did everything she could to break their fever and make the flu dissipate. By the end of the week, Minerva finally felt well enough to sit up and move around.

That evening she helped with the milking again, but her mom was concerned that she would overexert herself. "Please be careful, Minnie. You still aren't feeling the best." She glanced at Ida, lying on the couch in the living room, and spoke again, almost to herself this time. "This flu is more severe than I like."

Minerva wasn't worried about it. She still felt weak, but at least she could help again with the chores. At thirteen years of age, she always milked two cows, one of them being Becky with her short teats. But that evening when she carried the milk buckets, she thought they weighed more than they ever had before. She staggered into the milk house and set them down with relief. Surely after a night's rest, she would feel better.

But the next morning she ached all over. Every muscle in her body hurt, and she couldn't lie any way that felt comfortable. So once again she stayed in bed all day. Through the open door she could see Ida, also still sick, lying on the couch in the living room. In the afternoon Dad brought his sick daughters a little gift, a pair of sunglasses with horizontal stripes of light and dark brown decorating the frames. Minerva tried them on but soon laid them aside, feeling too ill to really enjoy them.

Mom came into the room, a small box in her hand. "I have some sugar puff cereal for you, Minerva. I'll put it here on this chair, and you can reach it from the bed."

As she left again, Minerva tried to pick up some of the cereal to eat. But somehow, her hands would not cooperate. From where she was lying on the couch in the living room, Ida watched Minerva lean forward even farther, trying to walk her fingers toward the cereal pieces. But try as she might, Minerva could not lift them to her mouth. Finally giving up, she lay back again and asked for a drink.

Mom brought a glass of water. Once again, Minerva tried to lift her arm to take it. And again it refused to cooperate. "I can't lift my hand, Mom," she said finally, close to tears. "My arms are so tired today. I can hardly swallow anymore, either."

Mom stepped closer and took her hand. When she let go, it fell back to the bed. A look of fear crossed Mom's face, and her voice was tighter than usual when she said, "Lie down on your back, Minerva." As Minerva obeyed, Mom lifted both of her arms. When she released them, they fell lifelessly back to the bed.

"I think you have polio, Minerva," Mom stated, her voice trembling. Turning, she hurried to the door. Dan had just arrived home from the Smith-Calhoun cemetery, where he had been helping to dig a grave. Now Mom called to him. "Dan, I think Minerva has polio. Will you go tell Dad right away?"

"It isn't that bad," Minerva exclaimed. "I'll feel better again soon, you'll see!"

There were tears in Mom's eyes when she answered. "I hope so, Minnie. I hope so."

Dan Gingerich had run errands before, but none this important. Though he biked as fast as he could along the road to where his dad and brothers were baling hay at Jonas Yoder's farm, the six miles seemed never-ending.

"Mom thinks Minerva has polio," he gasped to his dad when he finally reached him in the field.

Dad looked stunned. "Oh, no. Oh, no," he repeated, as if in a daze.

Dan nodded emphatically. "Yes! Mom thinks she has polio,

and she asked if you can come home."

"I'll come right away," Dad said without hesitating.

When Jonas Yoder heard what was happening, he offered them a ride home. As soon as Jonas stopped at the gate, Dad was out of the car and hurrying toward the house. When the others came inside, he said quickly to Dan, "Run up to the neighbors' and call our family doctor. Ask if he'll come out and examine Minerva."

Jumping on his bike once again, Dan sped away. He stopped at their nearest neighbors' home and asked to use the phone, but when they heard the reason, they requested that he wouldn't enter. They had newborn twins in the house and were afraid he might be carrying the disease. So Dan rushed in the opposite direction, heading toward their landlord Frank Cary's house. Hot wind whipped across his face and tears stung his eyes. Would Dr. Ingmire come in time?

As the afternoon wore on, Minerva's breathing became more difficult. It was hard work for her to get air. Jonas and Emma sat at her bedside, encouraging their daughter and praying as her breathing grew shallower and shallower. At last Dr. Ingmire arrived. He examined her quickly, his face grave. "This girl has polio," he said at length. "She'll have to go to the hospital immediately."

His words struck like a death knell to the family. The ambulance was called, and paramedics carried Minerva out on a stretcher. Her parents were allowed to ride along. As the ambulance rushed out the lane with its critically ill patient, a heavy cloud of fear descended upon those left behind. Would their sister come back alive?

The Children's Hospital in Columbus was nearly an hour away from Plain City. Night had fallen by the time the ambulance drove up to the emergency drive-through and stopped. In her haze of pain, Minerva was hardly aware of the paramedics taking her up to the second floor. There the nurses worked quickly, placing her in an iron lung that supplied life-giving air and forced her lungs to breathe. She fell instantly into a deep sleep, while her parents waited and prayed.

Morning came, and Minerva awoke to find herself on a foam bed. The iron lung she lay in was a big tube-like machine, similar to a propane tank, with bellows at the end to blow air in and out. The air moved back and forth inside the iron lung, like artificial respiration. Now she looked around groggily. *Where am I? What's going on?* Her head was outside the iron lung on a headrest, and she could feel air flowing into her lungs. Nearby she could see another iron lung, where a little boy was still sleeping.

The door opened, and two doctors came in. "How are you this morning?" one of them asked cheerfully, pausing beside her. "You're a very sick little girl, but we'll do all we can to help you feel better. Right now we need to do a little work on you."

The second doctor stepped up on the other side, and Minerva saw a clear plastic dome in his hand. Before she knew what was happening, he had clamped it over her head without explanation. What were they doing? Would they suffocate her?

She thrashed against the tight bubble in terror, wanting only to get out. As though from far away, she heard the doctor saying, "It's all right. You can breathe." They were opening the iron lung, and finally she realized that there was nothing she could do to escape. She grew still, taking sobbing gasps of precious air. She was indeed breathing, just like they had said.

The doctors hooked IVs to her body and checked all her vitals, asking questions the whole time. When had she first gotten ill? How had she started paralyzing? Minerva answered as best she could. It was all coming back to her now. "Where are my parents?" she asked. "Can they come up here to see me?"

"They aren't allowed to come inside this room," one of the doctors replied kindly. "But they can stand in the doorway." He smiled. "Your dad has been up here every hour to check on you and see how you're doing."

Minerva smiled faintly in response and closed her eyes. She was so tired.

CHAPTER FOUR

Hospital Time

August 1952

The cloud of fear hanging over the family at home grew darker. Their thoughts were at the hospital with their parents and young sister, and all were dreading what the future held. Noah and Ora were both married now, and with Lovina working at the Norrises', Fannie was the oldest girl at home. She felt the heavy weight of responsibility settling on her shoulders.

The first night after Minerva went to the hospital, Ida became delirious. She also had polio, but her symptoms had not worsened to the point that she had to go to the hospital. As the hours wore on, Fannie and Verna kept vigil over their youngest sister, doing all they could to break her raging fever. It was the longest night they'd ever known.

When morning dawned at last, both girls were exhausted. Standing by the window, Fannie watched the sun rise on the eastern horizon. Its beauty seemed to mock her burdened heart. She turned slowly. "I'll stay up with Ida for a while if you want to rest, Verna."

Verna hesitated but then nodded. "But after I get up, I'll let you sleep."

As Verna left the room, Fannie dropped her head into her

hands. "Oh, God," she whispered. "Please help us . . ."

The door opened, and Fannie glanced up sharply. "Lovina!" she cried. "I thought you were at the Norrises' house!"

"Fran brought me home this morning," explained Lovina, coming to her side. "I wanted to come as soon as I heard that Minerva is in the hospital. Fran didn't think I should because we don't know how contagious polio is, but I felt that I needed to. I'll be staying over the weekend."

She studied Ida for a moment. The small girl was sleeping now, her cheeks flushed. "How is she?" Lovina asked softly at length.

"Verna and I took turns staying up with her all night," Fannie answered. "She was delirious, but seems to be doing better now."

Lovina looked at her closely. "You don't look like you're feeling well yourself."

The concern in her older sister's voice brought tears to Fannie's eyes. "I'm so tired," she admitted.

"Why don't you go on to bed right now? I'll stay here with Ida." Lovina placed a gentle hand on Fannie's arm. "Please, Fannie. Go now and rest as long as you need to."

At her kindness, Fannie's tears spilled over. "Thank you, Lovina," she whispered.

It was a week before Ida began to recover from the polio, with no paralyzing effects such as Minerva suffered. The family at home prayed daily for their sister in the hospital while the oppressive cloud of uncertainty continued to hover over them.

Lovina stared out the bus window, hardly noticing the blue threads of the river through trees and shrubs lining the road. It was the second Saturday now since her sister had been in the hospital, and Lovina was planning to stay there for the night with her brother Dan. But her dread was growing with each mile that brought them closer to Columbus. "Everything has changed," she confided to Dan. "Nothing feels right anymore."

Dan brushed a hand over his eyes. "It's hard for everyone, Lovina. The polio epidemic is spreading over the whole country, and no one knows how it starts. Minerva is only one of many."

Lovina knew he was right. Every room on the second floor of the Children's Hospital held polio patients, many of them

The Children's Hospital in Plain City; photo taken around 1948.
Credit: Medical Heritage Center, Health Sciences Library, The Ohio State University

from the Plain City community. Quite a few were Amish and Mennonites. Some of them, like Esther Troyer and Loyal Farmwald, had been admitted before her sister. Now there were three children from Alvin Miller's family in the hospital, as well as Ervin Hostetler, Mary Jane Farmwald, and little Katie Plank, who couldn't walk anymore. There was also another Katie in the hospital, married to Jonas Kurtz. The Amish church hadn't held services for a while now. Not knowing how contagious the disease was, no one wanted to take the risk.

Polio was new to the doctors and nurses as well. They weren't trained for it and were learning daily how to treat their patients.

The whole situation was devastating for the Gingerich family.

What was ahead? They wondered if God would choose to spare Minerva's life or if He would take her home to glory.

Lovina and Dan found their parents in the hospital lobby. "The doctors said that Minerva is in very critical condition," Dad told them quietly. "She has great pain in her side that won't go away. The X-rays do not show that she has pneumonia, and they feel that her pain level is too high to be appendicitis. The doctors don't know what to think. They had scheduled an exploratory surgery for tonight, but then other doctors came in for a consultation. One doctor requested that they wait until morning and then take more X-rays." Dad's voice trembled. "They told us that she has only a fifty percent chance of survival."

"I went up to Minerva's room earlier today to stand in the doorway," Mom said. "Minerva was lying in the iron lung and could see me in the mirror above her head. She told the nurse, 'Let me see Mom one more time.' " Mom choked to a stop, unable to go on. Their tears flowed freely now.

"I don't want to ask too much of the Lord," Dad said huskily at length. "I pray that He'll see fit to spare Minerva's life and keep her with us. I will gladly take care of her, even if she is handicapped. But we do want the Lord's will to be done."

Let me see Mom one more time. The thought rang through Dan and Lovina's minds as they tried to sleep that night. When sleep evaded them, they walked the halls, hoping and praying that their sister would live to see the dawn of a new day. The grim shadow of death had never hovered so near.

Dr. Harding was the one who had suggested taking more X-rays of Minerva's lungs. In the morning, the X-rays were taken quickly, this time showing evidence of double pneumonia.

Over the next three days, the doctors drained fluid from Minerva's lungs. Turning her on her side, they used a small portable machine to breathe for her, placing its mask over her nose and mouth while they worked. Though they didn't show Minerva the long needle, she could feel its prick going between her ribs into her right lung. She hoped that the doctor holding her mask would not loosen his tight grip; she needed it to breathe!

When at last the doctors were finished, they had drawn out eight ounces of fluid. The next day they drew out four ounces. After the third day's two ounces, they put her on antibiotics to help clear out the rest of the fluid.

For the first time since she'd entered the hospital as a patient, Minerva started feeling better. Weighing only around seventy pounds before, she had by this time lost twenty-five pounds, which brought her to only forty-five pounds. "You're too thin, Minnie," Dr. Donaldson told her with a cheerful smile. "But now that the fluid has drained from your lungs, you'll be able to gain some weight."

Minerva looked up at him, her eyes big and dark in her thin face. "Oh, I'd rather milk a thousand Beckys than go through this," she said softly. "Becky is the cow I always milked at home. No one else wanted to." Her eyes grew wistful at the memory.

Dr. Donaldson sobered. "You have Dr. Harding to thank for saving your life, Minerva. He was the one who suggested that we wait until morning and then take more X-rays. If we would've gone ahead with the exploratory surgery, I doubt you'd still be alive."

As the doctor left the room, Minerva thought over his words. She hadn't known she was so close to death. Though she'd never met Dr. Harding personally, she knew that God had sent him to intervene with the other doctors' decision and save her life.

Over the next few days, Minerva drifted in and out of delirium. But finally the pain afflicting her body began to melt away, and the shadow of death lifted its heavy veil. As the days passed, Minerva hoped she would soon recover from her polio and be able to go home. Yet she did not improve. Her arms remained paralyzed, and she was still unable to swallow. The future looked dim.

CHAPTER FIVE

Wedding Cake Therapy
September 1952

Time always moved swiftly in the moments Jonas and Emma Gingerich spent together. Those moments were rarer now than ever before in their married life, as Jonas spent nearly every night at the hospital with his daughter. He felt burdened with the need to protect Minerva and be there for her as she faced the uncertainties of hospital life.

But at times duty called him home. On those days, Emma traveled alone on the bus to Columbus to spend the day with Minerva at the hospital. One chilly September morning, two weeks after Minerva had been admitted, Jonas stood by the door at home, watching for the bus as Emma donned her wraps. "I know you'll take good care of Minerva. I'll pray for wisdom and courage for both of you," he said, turning toward her. "And take care of yourself," he added with concern, noting the tired lines in her face.

"I'll do my best. Thanks for praying for us." The bus was stopping at the end of the lane now, and Emma hurried out. She found an empty seat near the back of the bus and slipped into it, thinking of how desperately she needed that wisdom and courage. Tears came to her eyes as she rested her head against the back of the seat, praying silently for strength to face the day ahead.

As she walked down the hall toward Minerva's room at the hospital, Emma tried to push away the dread that persisted on following her. It was always hard to see how frail her daughter had become, even though Minerva stayed positive through it all. She paused in the doorway, glancing in at the scene before her. A young nurse stood beside Minerva's iron lung, working through the port holes. Both the nurse and Minerva were laughing.

At that moment, Minerva glanced toward the door and saw her mother standing there. Her dark eyes lit up. "Hi, Mom!"

"Good morning, Minerva." Emma smiled back, drinking in the sight of her daughter's smile and the flush of color in her pale face. "How are you?"

"I feel good today." Minerva glanced at the young nurse, a twinkle in her eyes. "Guess what Gerry told me!"

Geraldine Elliot smiled as she turned toward Emma. "We've been trying everything we can think of to get your daughter to swallow," she explained. "I finally told her that if she learns to swallow before I get married in six weeks from now, I'll give her a piece of our wedding cake."

"I hope I can learn to do it." Minerva was beaming.

"Give it your best, Minnie," Emma said softly. She was thankful to see her daughter in good spirits, but her heart was still heavy when she headed down the hall toward the lobby minutes later. She found Katie Farmwald already there, standing by the window. She turned and smiled as Emma entered the room. "Hello, Emma. Did you visit Minerva already?"

"I did," Emma answered, joining her at the window. "She's happy this morning," she added slowly. "The nurse told me she would bring wedding cake for Minerva if she learns to swallow. That really brightened her day." She met Katie's kind gaze. "How is Loyal doing?"

Katie hesitated, her smile fading. "About the same." Andy and

Katie Farmwald's two-year-old son was completely paralyzed from the polio. "But God has been good to us," she went on. "Did you hear about the married man who died here yesterday? He was so big and strong, but polio took his life."

"I thank God for every day that He spares Minerva's life," Emma said quietly. "But I know each day could be her last. We have no promise of tomorrow."

Katie touched her hand with sympathy. "We must trust the Lord." Glancing out the window, she straightened abruptly. "What's going on out there?"

Emma followed her gaze. A steady stream of fire trucks poured into the hospital parking lot, their brassy red paint gleaming in the sunlight. "There must be a fire!" Katie exclaimed, her face blanching. "But where is it?"

I know you'll take good care of Minerva. I'll pray . . . Jonas's words rang through Emma's mind as she gazed out the window, and her knees went weak. She swayed and Katie caught her arm, quickly leading her to the nearest chair. Emma sank into it and sent a desperate plea heavenward for God to protect her daughter. Had Minerva survived the worst of the polio only to face this greater danger of a fire?

"Where's the fire?" The voice broke into Emma's thoughts, and she looked up. Katie was walking around the room, pausing at each window to look out. "If there is something going on, surely they would have told us by now," she said, glancing toward Emma. "I'm going down to the nurse's station to ask them. I'll be back in a minute."

Emma waited, her whole body tense. Terrible scenes of raging infernos, billowing smoke, and frantic screams of people trapped inside flashed through her mind. She was trembling when Katie returned. "They think there's a chance of a fire," Katie explained. "The trucks are here for standby."

Something snapped inside Emma. She couldn't handle the added potential danger on top of all the stress of the previous weeks. The threat of fire turned out to be a false alarm, but the shock on her mind caused her to suffer a nervous breakdown. For the next eight weeks she had to stay in bed, needing complete quietness and rest. At times it even took effort for her to breathe.

Heavy burdens lay on Jonas's shoulders. With his wife sick at home, crops to harvest, and frequent trips to the hospital to be with Minerva, he called on God many times for strength to get through the day. God never failed to answer his request, and He showered grace upon Jonas's laden heart.

Twilight was falling. Minerva gazed through the window, trying to imagine what was happening in heaven this night. The spirit of Randy Ernstein, her young roommate, had flown somewhere beyond the skies to rest with his heavenly Father forever.

Last evening the nurses had moved Minerva into the hall without explaining why. They told her later that death had come in the night to claim her friend. He had been such a sweet little boy, only three years old. Minerva ached for his family. As she watched the sky, the words of a familiar song brought comfort to her heart.

"No tears in heaven, no sorrows given, all will be glory in that land; There'll be no sadness, all will be gladness, when we shall join that happy band . . ."

"Minerva?" A nurse's soft voice broke into her reverie. "How are you feeling?"

Minerva turned her head. Geraldine Elliot—or Gerry, as everyone called her—was standing beside her iron lung. The care in her eyes made Minerva feel like crying. "I miss Randy," she said quietly.

"I'm sure you do." Gerry touched her hand. After a moment of silence, she reached into her pocket. "I brought something for you, Minnie."

Minerva caught her breath as Gerry held up a small music box. "Shall I wind it up and make it sing for you?" Gerry asked, smiling. Without waiting for an answer, she wound it up and set it aside. As sweet music filled the room, the nurse turned back to her. "This is yours to keep now. I'll wind it up to sing for you whenever you like."

"Thank you, Gerry." Minerva's eyes shone as she looked up at the pretty young nurse in her white uniform and cap. All the nurses were so kind to her. They often brought special treats and liked to play with her long black hair. Sometimes they bought bows to tie at the ends of her braids. They did everything they could to cheer her, and Minerva loved them.

"Fannie?" Verna stood in the doorway, her face serious. "I wish you'd come take a look at Andy."

Fannie turned from the sink. "His fever is getting worse?" Fear darkened her eyes as Verna nodded. She stepped into the living room, where Andy lay on the sofa with his eyes closed. Stopping beside him, Fannie placed a hand on his forehead. "Oh, I hope . . ." Her voice trailed off, but Verna knew what she meant. *I hope he doesn't have polio too.*

Ida was still recovering from her illness. With Minerva in the hospital and Mom still suffering from her nervous breakdown, the whole family was carrying a heavy load. How Fannie wished it could somehow be lighter. But she herself hadn't been feeling well lately.

Before the week was over, Fannie and Andy had both suffered light cases of polio. Although they did not become delirious or suffer major physical deformities, one of Fannie's legs would always be shorter than the other. But she was thankful for God's healing touch. If only He would see fit to heal Minerva fully too! Their omnipotent God could perform such a miracle if He chose to.

But she also knew that the Lord worked in mysterious ways. Perhaps He had other plans for her dear sister.

The day that Geraldine Elliot carried out her promise and brought a piece of wedding cake to Minerva in the hospital captured the interest of many people when they opened their newspapers.

"A promise was fulfilled and a pretty bride's happiness was

A PROMISE WAS FULFILLED and a pretty bride's happiness was shared by a brave little girl Saturday when Nurse Geraldine Elliott Joseph brought a piece of wedding cake to polio-stricken Minerva Gingerich. The little girl was unable to swallow when brought to Children's Hospital three weeks ago, succeeded only when "Nurse Gerry" promised her a piece of wedding cake. (Photo by Citizen Photographer Richard Garrett.)

The photo that appeared in the local newspaper.

shared by a brave little girl Saturday when Nurse Geraldine Elliot Joseph brought a piece of wedding cake to polio-stricken Minerva Gingerich," wrote reporter John van Doorn in a caption underneath a photo of Minerva and her nurse. "Attendants at Children's Hospital tried just about everything they knew to get the little polio-stricken patient to swallow," continued the article entitled "Slice of Wedding Cake Saved Her."

Her neck was paralyzed with bulbar and spinal polio. . . . None of the methods employed by the hospital attendants seemed to work.

The pleasant nurse assigned to take care of the little girl had watched all of the futile efforts. She too had tried for hours to encourage the youngster to swallow, but to no avail.

Finally, in desperation, the nurse said to the stricken child:

"I'm getting married in a few weeks, honey. If you'll try real hard to swallow, I'll bring you a piece of my wedding cake."

The youngster's eyes shone.

Her face became contorted with the tremendous effort she was making to swallow. Then she did it.

The little girl wanted so badly to share her nurse's wedding cake that she made herself swallow, attendants said.

Nurse Geraldine (Gerry) Elliot was married yesterday at 4:30 p.m. . . .

Right after the ceremony, a small reception was held at Gerry's apartment . . .

She and her husband, Max Joseph, cut the wedding cake [and] shared it with a small group of friends and relatives there. But Gerry was careful to set aside a large piece of the cake [and] wrap it in wax paper.

Then, only three hours after the wedding, Gerry and Max left the reception and went to fulfill the promise.

The 13-year-old polio sufferer was unbelievably delighted to see her nurse. Her eyes shone again as they had when she first learned of the wedding.

Minerva Gingerich swallowed the sweet crumbs eagerly, proud to show she was able.

And she nodded approvingly at Gerry's husband.

Max was content to play second fiddle to a little girl whose life had dwelt around a wedding cake for six long weeks.

CHAPTER SIX
Experiments

In the mirror on her iron lung, Minerva saw her dad appear in the doorway of her room. His eyes met hers, and he gave her a cheerful smile. She grinned back, wishing he could come over and talk to her. But she knew that he wasn't allowed any farther into the room.

She was so glad that she felt better now. Ever since the doctors had drained fluid from her lungs, she hadn't experienced the pain that had plagued her before. Eventually the nurses had moved her to a new room, number 215, and she was quickly growing to like it. Three other iron lungs and their residents were in the room, and she'd already gotten acquainted with all her roommates.

Marjorie Willock lay in the iron lung next to hers. The older girl had been a schoolteacher before she was stricken with polio. Now she needed constant care. The polio had made it hard for her to speak, but she was a good friend. If Minerva turned her head just right, she could see a poem taped to Marjorie's iron lung.

> I am the place where God shines through,
> For He and I are one, not two,
> I need not fear, nor fret, nor plan,

He wants me where and as I am;
And if I be relaxed and free,
He carries out His plan through me.

The thought-provoking words gave Minerva a desire to walk in God's will. Was her paralysis how God wanted to use her? How could she be a witness for Him?

A stir at the doorway caught Minerva's attention. Three nurses had passed her dad and were coming toward her. "It's time to wean you out of this iron lung, Minnie," Mrs. Archer said briskly. "I think you can breathe on your own if you want to." Without waiting for an answer, she opened the iron lung.

The flow of air reaching Minerva's lungs was abruptly cut off. Instant panic swept through her. "I can't breathe!" she cried out. "Please close it! Oh, please close it!"

Mrs. Archer stepped closer. "Minerva, you'll never get out if you don't try." But Minerva's face was white now, and she gasped for breath. Mrs. Archer hesitated, but then she glanced across the iron lung toward the other two nurses. "Help me close it," she ordered. As the iron lung was closed again, Minerva felt precious air flow into her lungs once more. Weak with relief, she sank back against the bed.

The nurses checked the other patients in the room and then left. Through her mirror, Minerva saw Dad stop Mrs. Archer at the door and speak to her in undertones. Though she didn't understand what he was saying, Minerva could tell that he was upset by what had just happened. A lump came into her throat as she realized how much her dad loved her and tried to protect her. Knowing how much her family cared about her encouraged her heart.

"It says here that we're going to start putting a tube through your nose that reaches down to your stomach to give you formula." The nurse looked up from the chart in her hand. "You can hardly eat or swallow, and that isn't good." Reaching out, she patted Minerva's dark head. "We want you to get well enough to go home again, Minnie. Lots of people are cheering for you. You're a special girl!" She smiled and moved away.

Minerva stared after the nurse, her mind racing. A tube through her nose that reached down to her stomach? It sounded awful.

Glancing toward the doorway, she saw Fannie standing there. Her older sister often came to the hospital to visit her. Now she motioned for her to step closer. "Tell Dad to come up here tonight," she said hoarsely. Fannie's eyes grew dark with concern. She nodded and quickly left.

As Fannie disappeared, Minerva turned her face to the wall and cried. What would happen now?

The nurses didn't feed her the formula that night, but Minerva knew it was only a matter of time before they carried out their plans. Her silent plea winged its way heavenward. *Oh, Lord, please help me . . .*

"Not so fast," Minerva pleaded, struggling to turn her head.

"You're okay, Minnie." As she spoke, the nurse put more formula into the tube that had been inserted through Minerva's nose. "Just hold still."

But Minerva knew something the nurse didn't. Some of the formula had gotten into her windpipe. It happened nearly every time they tried to feed her. "Not so fast," she pleaded again. This time the nurse didn't even seem to hear. Using a syringe, she put formula into the tube again, her fingers moving quickly.

It was too much for Minerva. She choked on the formula in her windpipe, her face turning white. The nurse took one look at her and rushed from the room. Moments later she returned with Dr. Donaldson, who came to Minerva's iron lung and pulled the tube out of her nose.

"Don't do this again," he told the nurse. "It's too dangerous. That tube was curled up and didn't even reach her stomach! The formula went into her windpipe and choked her."

Bending down, he smiled at Minerva and tugged her braids. "Keep it up, Minnie. You're a little fighter, and you'll make it all right."

Minerva tried to smile back. She appreciated his encouragement, but the nurse's effort to feed her formula had drained her. She felt so tired.

Finally left alone, Minerva remembered only one thing—Dr. Donaldson had said that they wouldn't feed her through the tube again. A silent prayer of thanksgiving formed in her heart as she fell into a peaceful sleep.

———

October 11 would always stand out in Minerva's memory. She could see the radiant blue sky through her window and the sun shone warmly. The room itself seemed cheerful when Ruth, a petite nurse's aide in a pink uniform, breezed through the door with a bright smile. "I have a surprise for you, Minnie-pooh!" Ruth had given Minerva the nickname after washing her hair with a bottle of Minipoo, a dry shampoo. "I'm just going to wheel you out of here," Ruth went on, grasping both sides of the iron lung. "Another patient needs your iron lung today. But first, the surprise is waiting for you in the hall."

"A surprise?" Minerva turned her head, straining to see past the door. "Is someone here to see me?"

Ruth laughed. "You just wait and see." She wouldn't say anything else, no matter how much Minerva teased her. As they headed down the hall, Minerva's eyes roamed everywhere. Then she gasped. "Verna is here!" she cried.

Her sister had tears in her eyes as she came over to the iron lung. "Oh, Minerva, it's so good to see you again!" She stroked Minerva's black hair and leaned closer, lowering her voice. "I came to tell you about your new little niece. Ora and Verna's baby girl was born just this morning. They named her Emma, after both of her grandmothers. What do you think of that?"

Minerva smiled and smiled. "I can't wait to see her!"

After Verna left, Ruth wheeled Minerva's iron lung into a small room. "We're going to put you on the tilt table while we take this iron lung to another patient," she explained. "We'll replace your iron lung with a new one and then move you back into the room."

The nurses had placed her on the tilt table before. It worked like a see-saw, lifting Minerva's body upright and releasing the pressure on her chest so that she was able to breathe better. But now Minerva felt uneasy. How long would it take the nurses to replace her iron lung with the new one? The second time they'd tried to wean her out of her iron lung, she had fainted. When she came to, she had sweated and chilled by turns. She hoped it would never happen again.

But that was not to be.

———————————————

"Minerva! Minerva, can you hear me?"

Jonas Gingerich, on his way up the stairs to check on his

daughter, stopped abruptly. That voice was coming from Room 215! He broke into a run, taking the steps two at a time as the call came again. "Minerva, can you hear me?"

Jonas halted in the doorway. Minerva's iron lung was open and Mrs. Archer was standing next to it, calling her name. "What's wrong?" Jonas demanded, fear making his tone harsh. "What happened?"

Mrs. Archer glanced toward him and held up one hand. "It's okay, Mr. Gingerich. Your daughter is fine."

Jonas looked from the nurse to the iron lung. He could see Minerva's face, pale and thin, lying against the headrest. Her eyes were closed. "Something happened," he stated, turning back to Mrs. Archer. "What is it?"

She straightened, looking offended. "Mr. Gingerich, you're the first person who's ever called me a liar."

Jonas refused to give up. "I want to know what you're doing with my daughter."

Silence fell as he waited for an answer. When the nurse spoke again, her tone was terse. "We're trying to wean Minerva out of the iron lung. She needs to breathe on her own if she's going to get well again."

Jonas understood now. "And she fainted when you took her out of the iron lung, didn't she?"

Before Mrs. Archer could answer, Minerva stirred and opened her eyes. Bending over the slight girl, Mrs. Archer adjusted her pillow and made sure she was comfortable. At last she came toward the door. Jonas stepped back, allowing her to pass through. Once in the hall, she stopped and looked at him evenly. "Mr. Gingerich, we're doing the best we can for your daughter."

When Jonas reported the incident to Dr. Baxtor later, the doctor explained more. "This is all new to us, Mr. Gingerich. We need to experiment on our patients so we know what direction to take in the future."

Jonas met his gaze steadily. "I'd appreciate it if you wouldn't experiment on my daughter like that again, doctor."

Opening the door of Room 215, Dr. Baxtor glanced back and nodded. "Understood, sir."

That was the last time they kept Minerva out of her iron lung for so long that she fainted.

"How are you doing this morning, Minnie-pooh?" Ruth stopped beside Minerva's iron lung, her smile reaching her eyes. "I bought some more bows for your hair."

Minerva grinned playfully. "How do you know I want them?"

Ruth laughed. "You're always glad for whatever we bring you and, well, I know it. I have dark green bows today."

Minerva glanced at the bows and felt the door of her memory swing wide open. They were just the color of the dress she had worn at her last Christmas program at school. So much had changed since that night. Back then she had never imagined that one day she'd be lying helplessly in a hospital, depending on an iron lung for air to breathe. She could swallow just a little now, mostly jello or sherbet. The doctors did not allow her to have ice cream or any other dairy products that would cause mucus.

But Minerva never dwelt on discouraging thoughts. Knowing that God was with her and that her family supported her was enough to keep up her spirits. Now she watched with interest as Ruth lifted one of her glossy black braids and looped a bow around its end. "Thanks, Ruth," she said softly. "They're beautiful."

Ruth smiled down at her. "I'm glad you like them. Today we want to see what happens when you're on a rocking bed," she went on, reaching for the other bow. "Now that you can breathe for longer periods of time when you're upright, we hope you can make it on the rocking bed while you're out of your iron lung."

"What's a rocking bed?"

"It's a tilted bed with a motor underneath, and it has a pivot in the center," Ruth explained. "It will rock you up and down, like a teeter-totter." Looping the last bow around her braid, she stepped back. "There! Now you're all ready for the day."

As Ruth stepped over to Marjorie Willock's iron lung, Minerva turned her head to watch. Normally a nurse was scheduled to stay in the room with them at all times. She hoped it would be Ruth today. This nurse's aide was so friendly and jolly that it was a delightful prospect.

Other nurses and doctors came and went as the morning progressed, but Ruth remained, watching over her patients and doing her best to keep them comfortable. She took a short break for lunch at noon.

Only minutes after Ruth left the room, Minerva heard a sound that made her heart stand still. One port hole on Marjorie's iron lung had not been latched properly and had fallen open. Her eyes wide and scared, Marjorie was trying to speak but couldn't.

Terrified, Minerva cried out, "Marjorie can't breathe! Help! Somebody, help!"

No one answered. Minerva called again, louder this time. Still, there was no answer. Her terror grew as she kept calling, praying that someone would hear her and come to the rescue.

Quick footsteps sounded in the hallway, and Mrs. Archer rushed into the room. As the nurse closed the port hole of Marjorie's iron lung, Minerva knew that if she hadn't been there, the problem could have been fatal for her friend.

As Marjorie took gasping breaths of air, Minerva sank back against her bed. One of her own port holes had fallen open once, but she'd moved her knee to the hole and plugged it until a nurse came and closed it again. Even though she couldn't use her hands, she was thankful that she could still move her legs. Marjorie couldn't even do that.

"I'm so glad you were here, Minerva," Marjorie told her gratefully when her breathing had returned to normal. "I might have died otherwise."

Minerva smiled back, her heart too full for words. Marjorie was already a close friend.

CHAPTER SEVEN

Giving Thanks

November 1952

"Shouldn't they be here by now, Mom?" Lovina looked out the window again, searching the road for the tenth time in five minutes.

Mom glanced up from where she was cutting an apple pie. "Judging by the time Ollie Christner left this morning, I think he'll bring her home in time to eat the noon meal. It shouldn't be much longer."

Lovina watched her mother for a moment as she turned back to her work. The weeks of recovery after Mom's nervous breakdown had been stressful for the whole family. It was so good to see her strong and healthy again.

Ida joined Lovina at the window, her brown eyes sparkling. "This is the second time I'll see Minerva since she's been gone. Last month when Dad took me up the back steps at the hospital to her room, I couldn't even go inside."

"We're all excited," Verna spoke up. "This is such a special day." She stood at the table, lighting two candles that had been placed in the center. The flames glowed in agreement.

Fannie, busy mashing potatoes, said nothing. But Lovina noticed the shadow that had fallen across her sister's face and felt her own joy dim. "I do hope Minerva doesn't get tired and quit breathing," Fannie had told her the evening before. Minerva's lungs had become stronger in the past weeks, and the doctors had decided that she was well enough to spend a few hours at home with her family on Thanksgiving Day. But now as she remembered Fannie's words, Lovina sent a silent plea heavenward for her little sister. *Lord, will you please help Minerva to make it through this day without a struggle?*

"Minerva will be so excited to see her sunshine box," Lester said, coming into the kitchen. "We put it on the library table, and she can open one gift today. But only one! She'll have to wait to open the others until the right day."

Lovina turned back to the fresh homemade bread she was slicing. It would be so special to have the whole family home for this day. Her two oldest brothers had come with their little families. Ora and Verna's baby girl was now a month old, while Noah and Fannie's little David would be celebrating his first birthday in December. With Minerva home, their family circle would be complete. They had waited so long for this.

"She's here! She's here!" Lester's sudden shout from the window resulted in a general stampede for the door. When Ollie Christner stopped his car at the gate, Dad was right there to lift Minerva from her seat and carry her to the house. Mom waited at the door, smiling through joyful tears. As she placed both arms around Minerva's frail frame, the others drew back, allowing their mother and sister a few moments alone.

Minerva's bed was positioned near the kitchen window, where she could watch everything that went on. Her dark head contrasted vividly with the white pillow, and her eyes shone as she watched her family gather around the table. Though Mom hadn't cooked the traditional turkey dinner, the meal was just as special, with crispy fried chicken, steaming mashed potatoes, and all the other trimmings. Pies baked to perfection completed the spread. "This feast looks fit for a king," Jonas declared, smiling as he sat down at the head of the table. "Let's have devotions before we pray."

Minerva watched her father intently as he paged through his Bible. How right it felt to be at home again, listening to Dad lead out in family devotions. "I want to read a portion from Lamentations 3," Dad said. "In verses twenty-two through twenty-six, it says, 'It is of the Lord's mercies that we are not consumed, because His compassions fail not. They are new every morning; great is Thy faithfulness.' "

His voice choked a little, and he paused. The family waited quietly. At length Dad cleared his throat and read on. " 'The Lord is my portion, saith my soul; therefore will I hope in him. The Lord is good unto them that wait for him, to the soul that seeketh him. It is good that a man should both hope and quietly wait for the salvation of the Lord.' "

Closing his Bible, Dad bowed his head, his voice soft as he began to pray. "Dear Lord, we have so much to thank you for on this Thanksgiving Day. We praise you for your faithfulness to us as a family. Thank you that your compassions are new every morning. Thank you for health and strength, and for allowing Minerva to be home with us today. Bless this meal and the hands that prepared it. Bless our time together, and may your will be done in our lives. Amen."

Minerva received excellent care that day, with everyone making sure she had plenty to eat and felt comfortable. She reveled in seeing her niece Emma for the first time. Little David was shy at first, but before long he was showing her toys with a sweet prattle that made her smile.

As the day drew to a close, Minerva looked forward to returning to the hospital. She was tired and longed for rest. Her parents joined her for the long ride back to Columbus. As the towering brick hospital came into view, Minerva couldn't help smiling. She was glad that she'd been well enough to return home, but it felt good to be back again.

By now, most of the Plain City patients had been released from the hospital. Minerva remembered the day that Katie Kurtz had stopped at her door and told her that she was going home. Her husband Jonas had been there too, his face shining with joy.

Minerva remembered their happiness now as she looked out the window. The hospital was a place of sickness, suffering, and death; she knew that as well as anyone. But it also symbolized hope, a place where the medical staff did their best to help the patients get well. Minerva was growing stronger every day. The iron lung had saved her life, and she depended on it now to help her breathe.

The nurses were still trying to wean her out of the iron lung. The rocking bed Ruth had described helped her to breathe, but it wasn't satisfactory. Her feet slid down as if on a see-saw when she tried to relax, and her knees buckled. But in spite of all this, Minerva felt secure in the hospital. Her iron lung supplied life-giving air, and the doctors and nurses looked out for her, treating her kindly. They all occupied a special place in her heart.

Her will to live was strong. God had blessed her with life thus far, even though it had sometimes looked as though the end were near. Now Minerva looked up at the wintry blue sky and breathed a silent prayer. *Dear Lord, thank you for your protection and good doctors. You are so good to me . . .*

The month of December was special in more ways than one. Minerva celebrated her fourteenth birthday, and on Christmas

Day she was allowed to spend several hours at home with her family again, like she had at Thanksgiving.

The New Year glided in with a glittering shower of freshly fallen snow, even whiter than the uniforms the nurses and doctors wore. As Minerva gazed out at the pure white landscape, she pondered the year that had passed. It had brought many changes to her life. Lively and active before, she was now helpless and dependent on the aid of others. Would it always be this way? She could only wonder.

"Minerva?" From where she was lying in the iron lung beside her, Marjorie's voice broke into her thoughts. "What are you thinking about?"

Minerva turned her head and met Marjorie's gaze. "I was just thinking back over last year. So much has changed!"

"It sure has." Marjorie hesitated. "I'm twenty-six years old, Minerva. I was a schoolteacher before I came here, but now . . ." She sighed a little. "I really hope I can go home this year. But life is so uncertain. My parents told me that in a few weeks I will take a private plane to Hanover, Michigan, for therapy."

"Really?" Minerva studied her friend for a moment. "Your parents care about you a lot, don't they?"

"They're doing everything in their power to help me. You know, Minerva," Marjorie sounded thoughtful now, "we have a good support team behind us. Your parents are doing all they can to help you, just as mine are for me."

"Yes, so many people care," Minerva answered. "The doctors and nurses, all the visitors who come to see me here, and the friends who send cards and flowers. Someone in Kansas even made a scrapbook for me." She glanced toward the wall, where the nurses had taped all the cards she'd received. People walking by in the hall often stopped to look at them.

The girls were silent for a moment. The stillness of the room was broken only by the raspy sound of air moving through their iron lungs. In the hall beyond the door came the faint sound of a child's laughter.

Minerva spoke again, her voice soft. "When I was home for Thanksgiving, I memorized a verse that I've thought about a lot ever since. 'It is of the Lord's mercies that we are not consumed, for his compassions fail not. They are new every morning; great is thy faithfulness.' " She paused and looked at Marjorie, a light shining deep in her eyes. "That explains everything, doesn't it?"

Marjorie didn't answer right away. "You're right," she said at last. "We can't even live without God giving us the breath of life. He holds us all in the palm of His hand."

CHAPTER EIGHT

Adjustments

January 1953

Fannie wiped the counter with her dishcloth one last time and glanced around. She could see Dad working at his desk in the living room. Ida sat on the couch nearby with a songbook, where she'd been singing for the past ten minutes. In her arms she held her doll, and in the small, white cradle at her feet lay Minerva's doll. It was a scene that made Fannie's heart ache. She knew that Ida didn't play much with her doll anymore. The nine-year-old missed her sister, who had always done everything with her. But now Minerva was in the hospital, and life had changed for all of them.

As the days passed, Minerva was gradually gaining strength. She had recovered enough to be taken out of her iron lung and placed in a wheelchair for part of the day. Since Minerva was feeling better and a lot of work needed to be done at home, Dad didn't go to the hospital as often anymore. This allowed Fannie and Verna to take turns going down every day. Normally they arrived in the afternoon. On the weekends when Lovina was home, she often went down too.

A glance at the clock showed Fannie that she needed to be ready to leave in an hour. Leaving the clean kitchen, she headed up the stairs to her room. At this time of day, the house was quiet. Mom and Verna were both resting, and her brothers were outside, spreading straw for the cows in the loafing shed. *Life has changed so much from what it used to be,* Fannie mused as she gazed unseeingly out her window. *It will never be the same again, no matter how much I long for it.*

Tears stung her eyes as she turned away. She could still hear Ida singing downstairs, with Minerva's doll in its cradle at her feet.

Laughter drifted through Room 215's open door, quickening Fannie's steps as she walked down the hall. Minerva's laughter was a heart-warming sound, making whoever heard it want to be right there with her. A nurse came out of the room, carrying an empty tray. Her eyes were twinkling.

Minerva was already sitting in a wheelchair next to the window, with an open Bible on the small table before her. A small cup with a straw provided a refreshing drink. She wore a flowered robe, and two long braids fell across her shoulders. As her gaze fell on her sister, her face lit up. "Hi, Fannie!"

Fannie came to her side. "How are you this morning, Minnie?"

"I'm doing okay. I just finished my breakfast, and they gave me eggnog to drink. Ugh!" Minerva shuddered, but there was a merry gleam in her dark eyes. "They didn't beat it, and it was slimy. Sometimes I gulp it down with a straw, but I couldn't bear to think of doing that today. I told my nurse's aide to throw it down the drain."

"Did she?"

Minerva nodded and laughed again. "Ruth always helps me get rid of food I don't want. Sometimes she'll eat it herself. Usually, though, the nurses just throw it out. Ruth brought me a glass of water right before you came in."

"What are you reading?" Fannie asked, glancing at the Bible.

"I was reading Psalm 23," answered Minerva, her voice softening. "I love this chapter. 'The LORD is my shepherd; I shall not want. He maketh me to lie down in green pastures: he leadeth me beside the still waters. He restoreth my soul.' " She paused, her glance skimming down the page. "Here's a verse I really like. 'Though I walk through the valley of the shadow of death, I will fear no evil: for thou art with me; thy rod and thy staff they comfort me.' " She looked up. "Isn't that beautiful?"

Minerva received comfort from Psalm 23.

The shadow of death. Fannie looked at her young sister for a moment, wondering if Minerva realized just how close the shadow of death was even now hovering near her. "Yes," she said softly. "It's beautiful."

Minerva changed the subject. "Some of the nurses are going to wrap me in hot packs soon. They're hoping it will make my muscles more pliable and help them to function properly."

"This young lady declares that she'll be walking in just a few weeks if we keep giving her all these treatments." The nurse Fannie had seen earlier came through the door, smiling. "But I think she still has a ways to go before she can walk!"

Minerva grinned up at her. "You're all taking such good care of me that I should be able to try soon. Right?"

"We're doing our best to help you reach that point," the nurse assured her, patting her dark head. "But it takes time." She glanced at the chart in her hand. "You have a few minutes to talk with your sister before we start with the hot packs." With a smile, she moved away.

"They put you through a lot, don't they?" Fannie asked dubiously, turning to her sister.

Minerva laughed. "I suppose they do. They're giving me therapy now too. They lift my arms one at a time and put them straight up to stretch them. Sometimes it hurts, but I'm not scared like I was when they tried to feed me formula through that tube they put in my nose. Sometimes I just had to cry when they told me they were going to do that again, and I'd pray for God to help me. But, Fannie, the longer I'm here, the more I know that God is with me."

Fannie, watching the quiet glow in Minerva's dark eyes, marveled at her faith. What she was facing now would be enough to shake even a strong person's faith. But Minerva, young as she was, had a connection with God that helped her to accept her circumstances cheerfully.

Mrs. Hanover and Mrs. Archer were the nurses assigned to give Minerva the hot pack therapy. They brought a large can with water that held soaked wool blankets steaming with heat, and they wrapped the blankets around Minerva's arms and chest. Next they covered it with plastic.

"It's hot!" Minerva exclaimed as the nurses stepped back. "It's too hot," she declared again, struggling to lift her back from the burning heat.

Fannie stood at the door, watching helplessly as her sister endured the pain of yet another medical treatment. *Will this ever be over?* How she longed to take Minerva away from this place. To see once again the young girl who skipped across green fields and flowery meadows, scattering sunshine and laughter—the picture of perfect health. Were those days gone forever?

The nurses continued with the hot pack treatment for a couple weeks. Though Minerva experienced pain from the heat every time, she never had blisters. Day by day she grew stronger, both in body and spirit. In a place where sickness and death were reality, her outlook did not change. She did not let anything get her down, which brought sunshine to a depressing atmosphere. Even though she could not be at home scattering sunshine and laughter, God was using her joyful spirit as a witness for Him in the hospital.

CHAPTER NINE

Step by Step
February 1953

The day came when the nurses moved Minerva to room 208, on the other side of the nurses' station. It was a pleasant room with three friendly roommates and a window that overlooked a park below. Minerva could often see children playing there.

Six months had passed since Minerva had come to the hospital. How completely her life had changed! As she looked out her window that morning, watching children play in the park, a startling thought came to her. *At one time I was just like them!*

She glanced at her lifeless hands lying on the bed. Outside in the hallway she could hear stirrings of hospital life, but her room was quiet. An idea took shape in her mind. She couldn't use her hands, but what about her feet? Could she walk? Her roommate June Roberts could, and she'd been stricken with polio too. Would it hurt to try for herself?

Minerva hesitated a moment longer before making up her mind. Slowly, carefully, she slid from the bed and stood up, determination giving her strength. *I'll show them I can walk!* She swayed and almost fell, feeling dizzy. This was the first time in six months that she was standing. Catching herself just in time, she waited for the dizziness to clear, then ventured one step forward. And another.

The door was only a few feet away now. She inched toward it, wobbling with every step. A couple steps more, and she was in the hallway. She looked ahead. The restroom wasn't far away. Feeling more confident, she headed toward it. If she could just make it to the door . . . ahh, she had reached it! She turned and moved back the way she had come, filled with excitement, even though her steps were still slow and wobbly. She was walking! She couldn't use her hands, but she could walk.

As she entered her room again, her roommates began to cheer. She lowered herself carefully on the bed and beamed at them all. "Can you believe it? I walked to the restroom door and back!"

"Good for you!" Phyllis called out. She was a sweet little girl, always sharing in others' joy, even though her own arms and legs were paralyzed.

"I won't do that again soon, though," Minerva said, sinking back against her pillow. "Once is enough!"

"I wish I could walk," Cecil said wistfully. Her limbs had also been paralyzed from polio, though her lungs were healthy and she didn't have a respirator.

"From now on, I'm going to let the nurses help me," Minerva declared. "I know I could've easily fallen without a nurse beside me."

"Well, that's what they're here for," laughed June. "In time you might be able to walk as well as I can."

Minerva smiled back. "I hope so."

The sun set over the city, painting clouds with vivid golden hues. Minerva gazed through the window, admiring how the tree branches outside made dark silhouettes against the sky. She had to laugh when a bird perched on one of the branches, cocking its head and peering into the room with curious eyes. It chirped and gave a saucy flip of its tail, then flew away again.

"How far did you walk today, Minerva?" Phyllis asked from the bed next to hers.

Minerva turned her head. "The nurses don't allow me to go very far yet. But I did see Loyal Farmwald. He's only three years old, and so cute! He saw me in the mirror above his iron lung and called for me to come in."

"He's the pet of this whole floor," June remarked. "Everyone bows to him."

"I met another little boy today too," said Minerva. "His name is George Warner, and his whole body is paralyzed. I also visited Donna—she's in a room two doors down from here. I didn't spend much time at any of these places, but I think they liked it. They were all smiling when I left."

"Maybe someday we can visit people together," June suggested.

Just as Minerva opened her mouth to answer, a horrifying *boom* sounded from somewhere below them. Window panes shattered into thousands of pieces at the impact, and glass flew across the hall into the girls' room. Within minutes, nurses were rushing through the halls, calling orders back and forth. "Get all the patients who are closest to the oxygen tanks and take them across the road to the nurses' dorm! Every floor needs to be emptied of patients!"

"The oxygen tanks in the basement exploded," Ruth explained hurriedly to Minerva as she placed her in a wheelchair. "Now there's a fire, and we have to get everyone out."

A fire! As Ruth wheeled her outside, Minerva saw fire trucks everywhere. Even though she could see no signs of the fire itself, there was activity all around her. A small part of the hospital had been damaged from the explosion, but no one appeared to be hurt. Doctors and nurses were transporting patients across the road to the nurses' dorm, and policemen had arrived to help. The traffic had also slowed down. Minerva watched it all in silence, her whole body trembling. Everything had happened so fast, she'd hardly had time to think about what was going on. But now reality sank in. What would happen if the entire hospital were to go up in flames?

But the firemen did their job well. The fire was under control before the hospital workers had moved the last patients out, and they were able to move everyone back to their rooms. Although it was a disturbing night for everyone, Minerva felt a great deal of thankfulness. God had protected them. She knew it could have been much, much worse.

Minerva's health steadily improved. Her walks became longer and she visited many rooms, learning to know the patients. It brightened their day whenever they saw her cheery smile and heard her voice ask, "How are you today?"

"You're always so happy," Norma Jean said one day. "And it's no wonder—you can walk. I can't do anything but lie here," she finished bitterly.

Minerva felt troubled at her words. Norma Jean was a young woman of twenty-two who had been going to school for nurses' training before she was stricken with polio. Now she was completely paralyzed. Minerva knew that she was struggling to accept her lot in life.

She glanced at Norma Jean's mother, sitting on a chair beside her daughter's bed. The pain in her eyes made Minerva long to do something to cheer them both. "Do you mind if I climb up and sit on the bed beside you, Norma Jean?" she asked.

"Go ahead." Norma Jean's mother moved her over a few

inches, and Minerva climbed up beside her. "A lot of other patients here are just like you, Norma Jean," she said softly. "You aren't the only one who can't walk."

Norma Jean moved her head impatiently against the pillow. "That doesn't make it any easier." She paused and sighed. "The nurses are planning to give me shots this morning. I can't stand when they do that!"

"They're just trying to help you get better and stronger," Minerva encouraged her. "When I first came here, I had to rely on an iron lung to help me breathe at all times. The nurses and doctors did their best to help me get better, and now I don't have to be in it so much. But I still get tired easily. When my sisters visit me, they usually tell the nurses when I'm tired and ask them to put me back into the iron lung. I don't know if I'll ever get to the point where I don't need it anymore."

Norma Jean's mother leaned forward. "But both of you girls are getting better. You're coming along!"

Minerva spotted Ruth coming toward them and grinned. "The nurses think I get into too much mischief, though."

"Don't you think we're right?" The nurse's aide winked at her as she stopped beside Norma Jean's bed. "I saw you duck and sneak past little Loyal's room today. It certainly looked like you were up to mischief again!"

The others laughed, and Minerva felt the color creep into her face. "He wasn't looking, and I was in a hurry to visit Norma Jean. But I'll visit Loyal on the way back to my room."

"I didn't know I was such a special person," Norma Jean said, and Minerva was glad to see the sparkle in her eyes.

"You are special," she declared, sliding off the bed. "And don't forget that! I'll see you later." The light in Norma Jean's eyes followed her as she left the room, warming her heart.

Ruth caught up with her in the hallway. "I appreciate how

you walk these halls and encourage the patients, Minnie."

Minerva smiled. "It makes me feel good too."

Tipping her head, Ruth studied her, her eyes twinkling. "Lots of people think you're quiet, but they don't know what a prankster you can be, Minnie-pooh."

Minerva laughed. "I'm just trying to be happy, Ruth!" Then she sobered. "God has been so good to me. When I walk these halls and see people who are paralyzed even more than I am, I realize that I have so much to be thankful for. Lots of them can't walk around; they have to stay in bed all the time. Why shouldn't I be happy?"

Ruth smiled and spoke softly. "Don't ever lose your joyful spirit, Minnie. It blesses more people than you know."

When Ruth brought breakfast to Minerva the next morning, she took a folded sheet of paper from her pocket. "I wrote a little poem about you last night, Minnie. Would you like to hear it?"

"I don't know." Minerva glanced at her roommates and pretended to be alarmed. "Should I be worried?"

Ruth chuckled. "Not at all. Listen."

There was a little girl named "Minnie Pooh,"
Lots of folk thought she had
little to do—
She was thought a quiet Miss
to be
By those who could not on the
inside of 208 see.
Little did they know that much mischief
she created—

And none of her pranks were ever
outdated.
We asked her one day why she
was so sappy.
She replied, "Oh, I'm just a 'being'
trying to be happy!"

"That describes her, all right!" called Phyllis, laughing.

"If you like, you can keep this," Ruth said with a smile. "I'll tape it on your bed here."

Minerva turned to watch as Ruth taped the poem to the headboard of her bed. Polio had changed her life, but with doctors and nurses to take care of her and friends all around her, she felt secure in the hospital world.

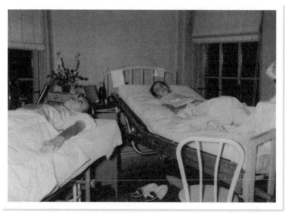

Minerva with the poem taped to her bed; Phyllis is on the left.

CHAPTER TEN

Where Is Home?
March 1953

"You say you made this in a craft occupational therapy class?" Lovina held up the small key chain made of copper and turned it over in her hand.

"Mrs. Gill helped me. We usually have these classes a couple mornings a week." Minerva's eyes shone as she spoke with her sister. She enjoyed seeing Lovina again. "It's supposed to stimulate our minds," she went on. "Sometimes I make things with my teeth, and other times I do finger painting. Mrs. Gill takes my hand and moves the paint around for me. That gets messy!"

Lovina smiled and set the key chain down again. "It's so good to see you feeling better, Minerva."

"Dr. Donaldson told me that they'll let me start going home soon for weekends," Minerva said. "I really like him. He always asks for a piece of the gum Dad keeps supplied for me. You can have a piece now, if you want. There's gum and Hershey bars in that drawer over there."

Lovina laughed. "Thanks, Minnie, but I think I'll pass. So you'll be able to come home soon for weekends? How excited everyone will be when they find out about that!"

Minerva smiled. "It'll be good to be at home more." She hesitated and then changed the subject. "How has it been going for you at the Norrises', Lovina?"

"Really good." Pulling up a chair, Lovina sat down beside her. "I keep busy, that's for sure! Their son George was getting all dressed up for a party when I left tonight." She paused, and her gaze searched Minerva's face. "How are you *really* doing, Minerva?"

Minerva knew what her sister was asking. How did she feel emotionally, deep inside where no one could see? "I feel blessed, Lovina," she said softly. "I'm stronger now, and don't always have to be in the iron lung. Even though my arms and hands are paralyzed, I can still walk! There are so many patients here who can't do that."

"Well, if you keep on like this, you might be able to come home for good this year," Lovina said, a sparkle entering her eyes.

As their talk drifted to other things, Minerva's mind stayed on her sister's words. *You might be able to come home for good this year.* Was she ready for that? There was security here at the hospital. She knew her family would do their best to care for her at home, but it simply wouldn't be the same.

Then she pushed the thought away. She didn't need to worry about it yet.

On the first Saturday in April, Minerva was allowed to go home for a visit. The day was sunny, with a crisp blue sky and fleecy white clouds. Minerva gazed out the car window, watching the countryside flash by. It was always good to see a change of scenery from the views the hospital windows afforded.

"So, Minnie, are you excited to be going home?" Ollie Christner glanced at her through the rear-view mirror, a smile in his eyes.

She beamed back at him. "Oh, yes. I can hardly wait to see my family again!"

"Well, everyone at home is certainly excited." Dad grinned at her from the passenger's seat. "Mom and the girls made your favorite dishes for supper tonight."

Minerva smiled and glanced out the window again. Her family always gave her such a royal welcome when she arrived home. What would she have done all these months without their support?

For the first time in seven months, Minerva was able to take her place at the supper table that night in her wheelchair. It brought back so many memories. The faces of her family all around her, glowing with happiness; the deep blue twilight through the window; the cheery light of dancing flames in the wood stove—all of it was enough to bring tears to her eyes. Here was love, family, and comfort; here was home.

Yet she wondered at the sense of reserve deep within, holding her at a distance from this world of family and home. In a real way, the hospital had become her world. She was excited to come home for a visit, but the thought of coming home to stay was a bit frightening.

She forgot about it, however, as the weekend passed by. On Sunday Mom stayed home from church with her, and Minerva reveled in spending time with her mother again. "I really wish I could go to the hospital and see you more often," Mom said, taking a sip of her morning coffee. "But it's hard to get away with everything that goes on here."

"So far, someone has been in to see me every day except three," Minerva said.

"We all care about you, Minnie." Mom paused as tears misted her eyes. "So much has happened, and it isn't easy to watch you suffer. Did we ever tell you about the false fire alarm last fall?"

"A false fire alarm?" Minerva hadn't heard about it before.

"I had come to visit you at the hospital, and I looked out the window to see all these fire trucks pouring into the hospital drive. Katie Farmwald was with me, and neither of us could see any fire." Mom took a shaky breath, and a tear slid down her cheek. "Oh, Minerva, I didn't know what was going to happen. I was so afraid . . ." Her voice broke off, and the tears came faster.

Minerva watched her mother silently, distressed to see her crying. "I'm okay, Mom," she said softly, leaning forward. "I'm still alive and getting stronger every day."

"I know." Mom smiled faintly through her tears. "And I thank God for keeping His protecting hand over you. You've been through so much."

Minerva thought over Mom's words. It was true that she had been through a lot. And as time went on, she was realizing that perhaps she never would get her full health back. But when she thought of all those patients at the hospital who were in worse condition than she, Minerva felt deeply thankful for how God had allowed her to heal. Though she wasn't the active young girl she'd been before the polio afflicted her, she had no doubt that this was how the Lord wanted her to live for Him.

Minerva thought she had never seen anything so beautiful as the spring that year. Cool breezes blew through the hospital windows whenever the nurses opened them, and fields bloomed with colorful wildflowers at home. The sun shone warm and bright, painting the forests a lush green.

But the morning she attended church for the first time since she'd been in the hospital, rain was falling. Minerva shifted in the buggy seat, her mood responding to the dismal weather.

The farther they drove, the tighter grew her feeling of dread. "Everyone's going to stare at me today," she said in a low tone to Ida, who sat beside her. "I wish I could have stayed home."

"Dad said you have to go," Ida reminded her. "You can't stay home from church."

Minerva glanced away. Dad had been kind but firm when he'd told her she had to go. But it was so long since she'd been to church that she wasn't looking forward to it. She hadn't seen many of the people in such a long time. How would they respond to her? Would the children stare?

Church that morning was held at a neighboring farm. While Dad tied the horse and buggy to a hitching post, the others went inside. Aunt Lizzie came bustling over right away to greet them. "It's so good to see you again, Minerva!" she exclaimed. "How are you?"

"I'm doing well," Minerva answered mechanically, aware of other ladies coming toward them. Most stopped to talk; others smiled and moved on. At last the service began. Reading the Bible and listening to the ministers share from the Word was like receiving a refreshing drink of water. Minerva's soul was filled, and she understood why Dad had said she must go to church. Here was a sanctuary where one could meet God and worship Him.

But after church, her worst fears were realized. Though the adults were friendly, little children stood directly in front of her wheelchair and stared at her. When she spoke to them, only a few responded. At length they drifted on, and despair threatened to settle upon Minerva. Where were the girls her own age? Were they too shy to come to her?

As if in answer to her question, two girls came around the corner and stopped beside her. "Hi there, Minerva!" The tallest girl's eyes twinkled with merriment. "I was so glad when I saw you here today."

"Katie Miller?" Minerva exclaimed, straightening in her seat. "I almost didn't recognize you. How you've grown!"

Her cousin laughed. "Well, it has been a while since we last saw each other."

"And here's Elma." Minerva smiled at the other girl. Elma Miller had been hanging back, allowing the cousins time alone, but now she returned Minerva's smile and stepped closer. "You must be feeling well if you're able to come home."

"I'm getting stronger every day." Minerva's eyes shone as she looked from one girl to the other. "It's so good to see you girls again. How are you doing?"

The rest of the time seemed to fly by. When at last they left for home, the rain had stopped, allowing the sun to come out. As its rays warmed the meadows, Minerva felt them surround her own heart. The world was beautiful again.

Minerva often traveled home for weekends that spring, staying from Saturday evening to Sunday. As spring turned into summer, the doctors began discharging her on Friday nights, allowing her a longer time at home. By now she slept in her iron lung for only part of the night at the hospital, and over the weekends she didn't have it at all. This made her so tired that she sometimes slept in church.

Though Minerva knew the doctors were trying to prepare her for when she could go home for good, time was slipping away faster than she liked. The hospital was a place of security. She depended on the doctors and nurses to help her, and she was surrounded by friends. Beyond the hospital walls was a new world. Would she be safe out there?

July 14, 1953, was a memorable day in the life of Minerva Gingerich. That morning Dr. Lyons came into the room, his smile wide as he boomed, "You can go home today, Minnie! You've improved enough that we've decided to discharge you and send you home for good."

Dr. Frank Lyons had always been one of Minerva's favorite doctors. She liked his cheerful ways and broad smile. But now, fear struck her heart as he added, "You won't have to take your respirator home with you, either. You've come a long way."

I won't have my iron lung anymore? I'm not ready for that. Minerva glanced down at her breakfast plate. She often asked for a couple pieces of bacon on the mornings they served it, but her appetite was suddenly gone.

"Alvin Hostetler is here with your father to pick you up," Dr. Lyons was saying. "I'll take you to the waiting room as soon as you're finished eating your breakfast."

"I'm finished," Minerva said abruptly, standing up. "We can go now."

As she walked through the halls with Dr. Lyons, Minerva stopped frequently to bid her friends goodbye. How she would miss them all. A number of nurses, hurrying about their daily tasks, paused long enough to give her a hug and wish her the best. At the exit doors, she stopped and turned, gazing one last time over the familiar infirmary that had been her home for nearly a year. Tears stung her eyes as she took a deep breath and spoke to Dr. Lyons. "I'm ready."

But she was strangely quiet on the ride home with Dad and Alvin Hostetler. Gazing out the window, she tried to keep the tears back. She was stepping into the unknown, leaving the secure hospital world behind. What did the future hold?

The sun was still low in the sky when Alvin Hostetler pulled into the Gingerich home driveway. Minerva felt her spirits rise as she saw her family coming toward the gate to meet them, with the smaller ones running ahead.

"They all look eager to welcome you home," Alvin said with a smile, glancing at Minerva in the rearview mirror.

"We've always looked forward to her visits," Dad said. "But now she's home to stay, and that's cause for great excitement." Opening the car door, he came around to her side. "Are you ready, Minnie?"

She grinned up at him and nodded. As Dad walked with her to the gate where her family waited, she tried to keep smiling. But the closer she came, the blurrier their faces grew. Only when she saw the tears in their eyes did she realize that there were tears in her own.

Of course, not all of them were there. Ora and Noah now had their own houses and families. But as they gathered around the table to eat supper that evening, the telephone rang. Andy jumped up to answer it. "Hey, Noah, Minerva's home! They discharged her today!" He listened for a moment and then turned to Minerva. "He wants to talk to you."

As Andy held the phone to her ear, Minerva spoke softly. "Hello?"

"Minerva?" Noah's voice came over the wire. "I want to tell you something. We have a baby girl, and her name is Ruth."

"Really?" Minerva cried, her dark eyes shining.

"What did he say?" Andy demanded, leaning closer.

"How does she look?" Minerva asked excitedly, ignoring her brother.

"She's tiny and has a head full of dark hair." Noah paused, and his voice deepened with emotion. "I'm so glad you're home again, Minerva."

Minerva smiled. "It's good to be home. I can't wait to see my new little niece!"

"A niece?" Andy snatched the phone away from her. "Noah, why didn't you tell me?" he exclaimed as the others began to laugh.

Minerva glanced around the room, peace settling over her heart like a comforting blanket. Even though life at home would be different from what it had been before polio, she belonged here with her family. And she could trust God to take care of her.

CHAPTER ELEVEN

In Search of Sleep

Summer 1953

The sultry day hardly provided even a whiff of fresh air. Minerva sat on the wooden porch with her sisters, watching them shell peas. "My, it's hot out here," Verna said to no one in particular.

Fannie glanced up from her work. "I'm sure the men are even hotter than we are. They've been working out there in the fields all morning."

"Ida and I took chocolate milk out to them earlier," Minerva remarked.

Gravel crunched under car wheels, breaking into the girls' conversation. The egg customer parked his car at the gate and got out, smiling as he strode toward them. "Imagine," he exclaimed. "Queens shelling peas!"

The girls laughed at his imagination, and Fannie stood up. "Can I help you, sir?"

After Fannie had left with the customer, Verna glanced questioningly at Minerva. "How are you feeling these days?"

Minerva didn't answer immediately. For a moment she gazed across the fields, watching the wind sweep through the tall grasses in waves. "I feel good," she said slowly. "And I'm happy here. Whether it's watching you girls work or taking cold drinks to the fields for the men, there's always plenty to do. I'm never bored!"

Verna smiled. "You're very observant, that's for sure."

Minerva's eyes shadowed. "I still shrink from going to church, though. My friends are kind to me, and I know that if I were one of the children, I'd probably stare at this girl who can't use her arms and hands just like they do. But I miss my friends at the hospital. Marjorie, June, Phyllis, Cecil . . . we had so many good times together. I miss the nurses and doctors too." She hesitated, gazing out across the fields again. "I'm glad that I can be home, but sometimes I feel like I left a part of my heart at the hospital."

"Well, you were there for nearly a year," Verna reminded her. "It isn't surprising." Tossing the last empty pea shell into the bowl at her feet, she stood up. "I'm taking this inside."

As Verna disappeared into the house, Minerva remained still, deep in thought. While she was happy here, the adjustment was taking time. Her life had changed so much that sometimes she almost felt like a different person. What did the future hold for her? Would her health continue to improve, or would it fail her again?

Looking up into the sky, Minerva breathed a silent prayer. *Thank you for being with me this far, Lord. Continue to work your will in my life. I know this is how you want me to be a witness for you . . .*

Gentle breezes waved tree branches in shadows across Minerva's pillow as she opened her eyes. For a moment she watched the morning sun highlight leaves of red and gold through the window. Autumn was coming, a season she had always enjoyed. But now the brilliance of the leaves hurt her eyes, and she had to look away.

The door opened, and Mom came into the room. "How do you feel this morning, Minnie?"

"My head hurts." Minerva's answer was so soft that Mom had to lean forward to hear. Concern flashed into her eyes, and she reached out to place a hand on her daughter's forehead.

"You look pale," she said, studying Minerva's face. "Didn't you sleep well last night?"

Minerva shook her head. She hadn't slept well at all.

"Why don't you try to get some sleep now," Mom suggested. "It might help you feel better."

Minerva didn't answer. She hoped Mom was right, but she couldn't help but wonder if this was only the beginning.

The severe headaches continued every morning, and before long Minerva was throwing up every night. Unable to breathe deeply enough to get sufficient oxygen to the brain, her breathing was shallow when she slept.

"I can work to breathe more deeply in the daytime, and I feel better then," she said one winter day as she sat at the kitchen table. Mom and her sisters were hurrying around the kitchen, finishing the last of the dinner preparations.

Mom paused in her work, glancing at her with concern. "How much sleep did you get last night, Minerva?"

"Just a few hours." That was a normal occurrence by now, and she'd been struggling to keep her drowsiness at bay all day.

"I'll let you lie down as soon as dinner is over," Mom promised. Dishing fried potatoes into a bowl, she brought it to the table. "Verna, will you tell the others that we're ready?"

Halfway through the meal, Minerva could no longer keep her eyes open. Without warning, her head fell forward, sending her plate flying across the room. Mom gasped and stood up. "We need to get her to bed. She's so tired that she's fallen asleep right here at the table!"

A hush descended over the kitchen as Dad quickly left the kitchen with his frail daughter. "Is Minerva going to be all right?" Ida asked, her voice small and scared.

"I hope so." Tears came to Mom's eyes as she cleaned up the kitchen floor and deposited the cracked plate into the sink. Minerva was home, but it was becoming obvious that she wasn't doing well. Would she eventually have to go back to the hospital?

By the time she was fifteen, Minerva's health was failing rapidly. Her nails and lips turned blue, and her feet swelled up to twice their normal size. Her kidneys were not functioning properly either.

"Take her back to the hospital," the family doctor said when he examined her. "She needs the iron lung."

So, eight months after she'd been discharged, Minerva returned to the hospital.

"Minerva! Minerva!" Nurse Ruth called again and again, clapping her hands sharply. The girl in the iron lung did not stir. Ruth knew she'd already been sleeping for a couple hours; Nurse Gerry had told her that earlier when they'd changed shifts. It was time now to give her patient medicine, but she couldn't awaken her.

Was something wrong? Ruth studied the pale face closely as she kept calling. The girl made no response, and at length Ruth turned and hurried toward the door. "Dr. Lyons, I can't get Minerva to wake up."

Dr. Lyons came at once. Standing beside the iron lung, he called, "Minerva!"

Minerva stirred and opened her eyes, turning her head toward the sound of his voice. "Now when the nurses try to wake you,

Minnie, you wake up!" Dr. Lyons leaned closer, concern in his eyes. "You must be dead-tired."

"I was just catching up on my sleep, Dr. Lyons." Minerva's dark eyes twinkled with amusement as she looked up at him. "I haven't been able to sleep properly at home for months now, you know."

"I see." Dr. Lyon's face relaxed as he nodded at Ruth. "Go ahead and give her the medicine. She's tired, that's all."

Drowsiness was already overtaking Minerva again as Ruth stepped to her side. Swallowing the medicine obediently, she closed her eyes and drifted back to sleep.

Minerva was in the hospital for two weeks before the doctors sent her home, with orders to return three evenings a week to strengthen the muscles in her lungs—or, as Dr. Lyons put it, "to blow out the cobwebs."

But it didn't seem to help. That spring Minerva often visited Loyal Farmwald's home, using his respirator to help her breathe. Little Loyal had also been discharged from the hospital and seemed to be doing well.

Minerva's health, however, was failing once again. Her feet started swelling, and her nails turned blue. "I think she needs an iron lung at home," Dr. Ingmire said when he examined her. "What do you think, Dr. Bunde?"

The student doctor stepped closer, his brow furrowing. He'd been present during Minerva's last two weeks at the hospital, and had come with his wife to visit her the evening Dr. Ingmire arrived. Now he listened to the shallow, raspy sound of Minerva's breathing and nodded. "Yes, she needs an iron lung at home. Otherwise she won't be able to stay there."

The evening Dad and the boys set up the iron lung in her room, Minerva stood in the doorway to watch. "The iron lung is called a respirator," she said to her sisters as they gathered around her. "A Drinker-Collins."

"Drinker-Collins?" Verna repeated blankly.

"These two men got together and designed it," Minerva explained. "Drinker and Collins were their last names." She stepped closer, surveying the large cream-colored iron lung. "I like this one better than the iron lung I had at the hospital."

"It belongs to the polio foundation, right?" Fannie asked.

"They all do," she answered. "When the polio epidemic first started, President Roosevelt had polio too. Nurse Gerry told me that he made an organization called the March of Dimes. People were supposed to donate to this fund, and it brought in lots of money for the polio people."

"A lot of people got aid from that," Mom added. "All the hospitals were loaded with patients."

"What do you think, Minerva?" Dad asked, turning toward her. "Is the iron lung in a good place here against the wall?"

"It's fine, Dad. Thanks so much!" Minerva looked around at her family, love swelling in her heart. They had supported her through thick and thin, and they were so thankful that she could be home. Now that she had the iron lung and didn't have to worry about getting enough oxygen to breathe, she could take her place among them, knowing she was home to stay.

CHAPTER TWELVE

Milestones

Spring 1954

The sun was setting in a splendor of pink and lavender toward the west, and merry birdsong filled the air as Minerva watched Mom and her sisters working in the garden. She loved this hour of evening, when the heat of the day had cooled to refreshing breezes.

"Lovina should be home soon," Ida remarked as she reached the end of her row near Minerva. "It seems it's been awhile since I've seen her."

Minerva glanced toward the road, but there was no vehicle in sight. Lovina had quit her job at the Norrises' and was now working for a couple named George and Betty Schmidt. The weekends she was home did indeed seem few and far between. "Lovina said once that she is always so ready to come home," she said. "But she likes her job."

Ida pulled another weed and then stood up. "Is it okay if I go to the house for a drink of water, Mom?" she called.

"That's fine." Mom glanced up briefly. "You can bring the rest of us water too."

"Sure." Ida turned to Minerva. "Want to go with me?"

As the girls walked toward the house, Minerva glanced around, taking a deep breath. "Oh, smell the honeysuckle! It's wonderful, isn't it?"

"May is almost over," Ida said, stopping to pick a daisy. She wiggled her bare toes in the grass and laughed. "I'm so glad that school will soon be out for the summer!"

Reaching the door, Minerva stood back to let Ida open it. As they entered the house, she glanced back. "Why, there's Lovina! Betty must have just dropped her off." She straightened for a better look. "What's that on her hand?"

Ida followed her gaze to where their older sister was walking toward the front door. Then she gave a little gasp and hurried forward. "Lovina! What did you do to your hand?"

As Lovina came inside, she held up her hand for the girls to see. It was wrapped tightly, but some blood had begun seeping through the bandage. "Betty had a built-in hutch with doors, and I wanted to put a strip of wood across a shelf to set up plates," she explained. "Ora had been doing a little carpentry work there, and he left behind some of his tools when he went home. I found a jointer-planer that I thought I could use. But I got my hand in the jointer, and it cut off part of my thumb." She winced as she pulled out a chair and sat down. "I think the doctor needs to look at it."

"I'll go get Mom," Ida declared, running out the door.

This time it was Lovina who entered the hospital as a patient instead of Minerva. The jointer-planer had cut off the tip of her thumb, and she needed surgery. But she was able to come home again the next day, declaring, "That's the last time I'm using a jointer-planer." Minerva had to smile, but she felt glad that nothing worse had happened. Lovina was a special sister.

"Here we are," Ollie Christner announced, parking the car in front of the gift shop. Minerva shifted in the backseat, her dark eyes taking in everything. Before today, she'd never had the chance to roam the city of Columbus and view its hustle and bustle firsthand. But now she was going shopping with her parents and Ida.

Sliding out of the passenger's seat, Dad came around to her door. "Be very careful when you get out, Minerva," he instructed. "I don't want you to fall!"

Minerva slid slowly from her seat, breathing a sigh of relief when she stood on firm ground. "Are we going into the gift shop now, Dad?"

"I actually wanted to go somewhere else first," he said, glancing through the gift shop's window. "Would you and Ida rather stay here while Mom and I go across the street?"

"Oh, could we?" exclaimed Ida.

"We'll ask the clerks if they're okay with it," he decided. Opening the door, he approached the counter. Seconds later he was back, smiling. "They said it's fine."

The gift shop's shelves were filled to the brim with enticing items. As the girls walked inside, they smiled shyly at the two ladies behind the desk. "How are you girls doing?" one of them asked, standing up from her chair.

"We're fine," Ida answered. "Do you mind if we look around?"

"Go right ahead." She smiled cheerfully. "And while you're at it, you can both pick out something that you can have for free."

Minerva's eyes lit up. "Thank you!" She followed Ida down the aisle, stopping at a shelf where cups and saucers were displayed. "Come look at this set, Ida," she called to her sister.

"It's tiny!" Ida exclaimed, coming to stand beside her. "Shall I hold it up for you to see it better?"

Minerva nodded, and Ida reached out to pick up the small cup and saucer. "I love that cranberry color with gold around the edge," she said, turning it over.

"The lady said we can pick something out," Minerva reminded her. "I think I'll choose this."

"Let me carry it for you," said Ida. "You might have carried a typewriter to Dad last night, but I want to make sure you don't drop this!"

Minerva grinned. The night before she had carried a typewriter in its case downstairs to Dad, who was working at his desk and too busy to get it himself. He had been so surprised!

She held out her hands, examining them closely. She could also open a drawer by throwing up her arm and aiming for what she wanted. But even though there was some strength in her hands, she doubted she would ever regain their full use.

Ida's voice broke into her thoughts. "I saw something over here." Leading the way to another shelf, she picked up a small ceramic bear figurine. "Isn't this the cutest thing?"

"It could break," Minerva cautioned as Ida picked it up.

"I'll take good care of it," Ida assured her. "Come on, let's look around the rest of this store."

When the girls returned to the front of the gift shop, they showed the clerks their treasures. "That is a *demitasse*," one of the ladies said as Ida held up the small cup and saucer Minerva had picked out. "*Demitasse* is the French word for 'half-cup,' and it usually refers to coffee."

Minerva laughed. "I'm afraid I don't drink much coffee."

"That kind of coffee is usually strong," the clerk said, and then she hesitated. "I was wondering if . . ." She paused again, as though searching for the right words. "I've noticed that you have limited use of your arms and hands. Do you mind if I ask what happened?"

"It's okay." Minerva felt shyness steal over her, but she understood this lady's curiosity. "I was stricken with polio when I was thirteen, and my arms and hands were paralyzed."

"I'm sorry," the clerk said sincerely. "I'm sure that was hard."

"But I can still walk!" Minerva smiled. "Many patients at the hospital were worse off than I was."

"Well, someone was looking out for you," the clerk said as the door opened to allow more customers inside.

"It was the Lord," Minerva answered. "And He is still watching over me."

As they left the city late that afternoon, Ollie Christner drove past Children's Hospital. Minerva turned her head, watching its towering walls until the building vanished from sight. Columbus held many memories, both good and bad. But she did not regret her time in the hospital, for her experiences there had drawn her closer to God than ever before.

On the morning of her sixteenth birthday, Minerva looked out her window to see pure white snow sparkling in the sunlight. Just like that unmarred snow, the year ahead stretched before her like a clean white sheet. What would fill the pages of this chapter in her life?

"Minerva? Are you awake?" Mom came into the room, smiling. "Happy birthday!" She helped Minerva out of the iron lung and then picked up a comb from the nearby bureau. "Here, sit on this chair while I comb your hair. Your friends are coming tonight for your birthday party, so we have a busy day ahead of us."

Minerva found a place in the kitchen to watch Mom and her sisters as they cleaned the house and baked special delicacies for the evening meal. The delicious aroma of chocolate cake was filling the house by the time Dad brought home a box of ice cream from town. "Hopefully this will be enough," he said.

"Those schoolgirls will have big appetites!"

Minerva smiled. Her friends from school would be getting off the bus at their house later on. Some of her cousins were also coming. She could hardly wait.

At last the school bus stopped in their driveway, and six girls flocked to the house. One by one the other girls arrived, talking and laughing as they gathered in the living room around Minerva. Her cousin Katie came in last, an extra sparkle in her eyes. "I brought a little gift for you," she said, placing the wrapped gift at Minerva's feet. "Happy birthday!"

Minerva watched closely as Verna unwrapped the gift. "Why, it's a dress!" her sister exclaimed, lifting the soft folds of blue material in her hands. Slitting open the card, she showed it to Minerva. "It's signed by all your friends, Minnie."

Minerva's voice choked a little as she thanked the girls. A movement at the doorway caught her attention, and she turned to see Mom coming into the room, carrying a cake with sixteen candles. As everyone joined in singing "Happy Birthday," Minerva bowed her head, not wanting anyone to see the tears in her eyes. For the past two years she had been too ill to enjoy her birthday much. It was special to celebrate it this year in better health, with friends gathered around her.

It took two tries for Minerva to blow out the candles, and when at last the flames were out, her friends cheered. They cheered again when the first piece of rich chocolate cake with white frosting was handed to her. "You're the honored one tonight," said Katie, laughing. "Shall I sit beside you and feed you?"

"I don't mind." Minerva smiled as she looked around the room. A new era of her life was starting now as she joined the young folks, but she wasn't the typical excited sixteen-year-old. Her health did not allow her to live like other young girls. Still, she looked forward to spending more time with her friends.

Dad and the boys came in from milking soon after the party was over. While Mom and Minerva's sisters washed the dishes, Dad came to the doorway. "You girls all need to get into Minerva's iron lung," he announced jovially. "It will help you get a feel of what her life is like."

Minerva grinned. Dad didn't like to get into the iron lung himself, but he always liked to watch how others reacted to it. When some of the girls protested, Dad shook his head firmly. "You're all going to try it!"

One by one, Minerva's friends climbed into the iron lung, lying on the foam bed as Dad closed it up. "Breathe with it!" he called. "You've got to breathe with the iron lung!"

One girl failed to comply with his directions and had to be taken out quickly. "Think where Minerva would be if she were that apprehensive!" Dad said, giving a big laugh. Minerva joined his laughter, and after a surprised moment, all the other girls laughed too. The iron lung was their friend's very life, and getting into it helped them realize this more than ever.

Minerva in the iron lung.

A holy hush fell over the church as the baptismal applicants filed to the front. Five girls, dressed in simple black dresses and radiating quiet peace in their eyes, knelt down to receive the sacred baptism of water. "Upon the confession of your faith, I baptize you in the name of the Father, the Son, and the Holy Ghost," bishop John Plank said as he cupped his hands on top of Minerva's head.

Katie Miller, Mary Troyer, Elma Miller, and Anna Gingerich knelt next to her, their presence a gentle promise. After this day, they would all be sisters in Christ. Joy filled Minerva's heart as she lifted it to the throne of grace. She had given her life to the Lord, and this day she was publicly vowing to serve Him and be His daughter forever. *Oh, Lord,* she breathed silently, *use me in any way you choose. I want to live my life for you.*

CHAPTER THIRTEEN

The Family Grows

On a cold, blustery day in November of 1955, Dan married his beloved Anna. Nearly a year later, Verna joined hands with Abe Troyer for life. Fannie and Ervin Hostetler were married the next March, leaving home an emptier place than it had ever been before—yet filled to the brim when they all came home.

Amid all these changes and adjustments, the familiar shadow of anxiety descended over the Gingerich family as the year of 1960 dawned. Lying in an iron lung at the hospital on that cold January day, Minerva couldn't help but think how fragile life really was. Though it was nothing new for her to get a cold in the winter, it had caused pneumonia this time. But she was receiving good care. Mom and Lovina often placed her head under a tent and used a humidifier to loosen her mucus. The steam from the humidifier helped her to breathe better.

The door opened and her brother Lester came into the room. "How are you this morning, Minerva?" he asked cheerfully, pausing beside her bed.

"I feel better than I did." Minerva smiled up at him. "What's been happening at home?"

Pulling up a chair, Lester sat down beside her. "Just the usual. Work and more work!" He grinned and leaned back in his chair.

"I hope you come back home soon, Minerva. Ida's been trying to sew a new dress this week, but she's lost without you."

Minerva laughed. "Oh, Ida knows how to sew mostly on her own by now." Ida had learned the skill of sewing from Minerva, who'd watched her older sisters sewing so often through the years that she knew exactly how to sew every seam. Ida was used to Minerva pointing at the seams with her foot and saying, "No, that isn't right! You do it *this* way!"

Now Lester's dark eyes twinkled. "Even though you've never sewn a dress yourself, you're a good teacher, Minerva." His smile faded as he turned to face her. "How are you feeling these days?"

"Dr. Donaldson was in this morning and told me that I should be able to go home this week yet," she answered. "I'm ready to leave this place. I don't mind the hospital, but I'd much rather be at home where I belong."

"There was a time when you weren't sure you wanted to come back," Lester reminded her.

Minerva didn't answer immediately. "That seems like a long time ago," she said at length.

"Well, I guess it has been," he said thoughtfully. "A lot has happened since then. Dan, Verna, and Fannie are all married now. Andy is dating Judy. Sometimes home seems rather empty."

"What about you, Lester?" Minerva glanced up at him, a sparkle of interest in her dark eyes. "Is there someone special in your life?"

"Listen to her!" Lester said to the ceiling. "She's lying here sick in bed, and asking if I have a special friend!"

"I told you I'm feeling better. And you do have something to tell me; I can see it in your eyes!"

He laughed again and leaned back in his chair, crossing his hands behind his head. "Well, what I have to say is probably different from what you think. Minerva, if I ever start dating, there is one thing I would want to settle with my girlfriend right away. Depending on what she says . . ." His voice trailed off.

Minerva watched her brother for a moment. "What are you talking about, Lester?"

"When I was in tenth grade, I felt that God was calling me to go on the mission field," he answered quietly. "I don't know where I'll go, or when, but if I ever start dating a girl, I want to ask her from the beginning if she would be comfortable going with me to the mission field. This is very important to me."

It took a moment for his words to sink in. "Oh, Lester! You mean you might leave our family and go overseas to the mission field sometime?"

"I can't ignore God's calling," he answered simply. "But I'm trusting Him to lead me. I know He'll show me where I am to go."

When at last Lester stood to leave, Minerva asked teasingly, "So what girl are you hoping will go to the mission field with you?"

Lester grinned. "You'll have to wait and see. Take care now, and I hope you come home again soon."

"Goodbye, Lester."

Lester and Sarah Kurtz were married on October 28, 1961, when autumn cloaked the trees with brilliant hues of red and gold. As she watched the young bride and groom, Minerva wondered what was ahead for them. Sarah had promised to stand beside Lester for life and cleave to him as long as they lived. Where would God lead them in the future?

Only a few days after the wedding, Hurricane Hattie swept through the seaport of British Honduras hundreds of miles away. "Over one tenth of Belize City's four thousand people were left homeless from the hurricane," Lester shared with his family one evening when he and Sarah stopped in for a visit. "The Amish Mennonite Aid mission board has agreed to help the hurricane refugees for two years. Their headquarters will be in the barracks of a little village named Hattieville." He paused and met Dad's gaze. "Dad, the AMA board has asked us to go down there. Sarah and I have both prayed about this, and we feel that God is leading us to go."

Dad looked from one to the other, tears in his eyes. "We wish you God's blessings as you go and serve Him there."

May's fragrant breezes serenaded the morning that Lester and Sarah boarded the two-motor prop plane bound for Belize. Only twenty-one and twenty-two years old, the couple's commitment to God was strong and sure. As she watched the plane lift into the air, tears misted Minerva's eyes. She would greatly miss her brother and sister-in-law. But their families had to let them go; God had work for them elsewhere.

In May of 1962, a young man named Dale Burkholder came to live with the Gingerich family. He and his sisters had been left homeless after their mother died, living temporarily with their older married sister in Holmes County, Ohio. But when Pauline and her husband Loyal moved to Plain City, there wasn't enough room in the new house for everyone, so they asked and received permission to let Dale stay with the Gingeriches.

Fifteen-year-old Dale quickly became Jonas's right-hand helper on the farm. The Gingerich family moved to another farm in March of the next year, trading homes with Noah and Fannie's family on the same day. The house was located close to the road that led to the town of Plain City.

Over the years, the Amish community in Plain City had dwindled. Very few Amish youth were left, and the girls often joined the Amish Mennonite youth for activities such as group singing. They usually rode to these singings with Dale, who was not Amish, but sometimes the Kurtz girls stopped in with their car to pick them up. Rosa, Mary, and Bertha, who were their sister-in-law Sarah's younger sisters, lived north of them and came right past their house. The girls quickly became close friends.

"Why don't you all come in tonight?" Lovina invited one evening as the two sets of sisters arrived back at the Gingerich home after an evening of ministry in Columbus. "We can have a snack and visit for a while."

"Sounds like fun," enthused Rosa. Parking the car, she slid out and went around to Minerva's door. "Be very careful," she cautioned. "I don't want you to fall!"

Minerva laughed. "You sound like my Dad. He always warns me to be careful when I go somewhere."

"He's been doubly concerned since she broke her hand," Lovina said, closing the car door.

"I remember that." Bertha glanced at Minerva. "You were getting into someone's van when you tripped and fell on your hand, right?"

Minerva nodded. "I saw I was falling and threw back my head so it wouldn't hit the floor. I went down on my knee then, and my hand was under my knee. But I didn't know until later that I had broken my hand."

"I'm just thankful that you don't fall very often," Lovina said, leading the way to the porch. "Come on inside, girls."

Their parents were in the living room when they came in. "So you made it home again," Mom said with a smile, glancing up from the magazine she was reading. "How was your evening at the city mission?"

"A lot of people attended tonight," Minerva said.

"Those people have to be there for the church service if they want a free meal, and I'm glad to serve it to them," Rosa commented. "But sometimes I wonder how effectively we're reaching them for Christ."

"They always seem touched when we sing for them afterward," Mary reminded her.

"Keep sowing the seed," Dad encouraged, laying aside his magazine. "You young people are doing a good work at that city mission."

"Sometimes I think that we receive the greatest reward," Lovina said thoughtfully. "When we go to places like the city mission, cottage meetings, or the Girls' Juvenile Detention Center, I always feel so blessed when we come home. I know that I've done something for God, and perhaps a life will be changed."

They were silent for a moment. Then Mom stood up and moved toward the kitchen. "Why don't you all come out here for a little snack? We have plenty of pie."

"Thanks, but we'd better not," said Rosa, glancing at her watch. "It's getting late and we need to go home." Opening the door, she stood back to let her sisters file through and gave a cheery wave. "See you later!"

Minerva followed Lovina to the kitchen, where Mom dished a piece of pie onto the plate. "Sit down at the table, Minnie, and Lovina will feed you," she said, setting the plate on the table. "Do any of the rest of you want pie?"

"I'll take a piece," called Ida. Stepping into the kitchen, she glanced out the window. "Look at that! The girls are coming back in."

She had barely spoken the words before the door opened.

Laughter swirled in with the Kurtz sisters as they came inside, and Lovina stood up. "We thought you had left already! Did you want some pie after all?"

"Well, they asked why I said we should go home," Rosa admitted, flushing a little. "They wanted some of that pie! So we decided to come in again. I hope you don't mind," she added to Emma.

"Of course not! Sit down, and we'll serve you," Mom said, bustling toward the counter. "It won't take long."

As Rosa sat down across from her at the table, Minerva grinned at her. "That's a Kurtz for you, to do something like this."

"Hey!" exclaimed Rosa with mock indignation. "My sisters were the ones who wanted to do it!" Then she laughed, and Minerva laughed too, knowing that Rosa was only teasing. The outgoing girl was a true friend who was always a fun companion.

"Hey, what would you girls think of going up to Holmes County with me?" Dale asked one night at the supper table. "I'd like to visit the community where I grew up."

"Sounds like fun to me," said Ida, her eyes alight with the idea.

"I was thinking I'd take my younger sister Mary Ellen along too. Is that all right with you, Jonas?" Dale glanced at Dad.

Dad smiled. "Sure. Just be careful."

Early the next Sunday morning, they drove to Holmes County and attended Dale's former church. After a picnic lunch in the afternoon, Dale took the girls to see the graveyard where his mother was buried, stopped in at the school, and drove past his old home place.

"This community brings back a lot of memories," Dale said when they finally started back to Plain City. "It's almost like coming home."

Mary Ellen nodded. "I hope we can come back again sometime."

"Do you feel at home in Plain City?" Minerva asked.

Dale grinned. "As long as I can tease you!"

They all laughed at that. Dale certainly was a tease, tweaking Minerva's nose when she lay in her iron lung, or putting his hat on her head when she watched him work in the field. He was like a brother to them all.

"Seriously, though," Dale said, "I'm thankful for how God has worked things out since Mom died. Even though I can't live with my sisters, I feel like He's given me a good life."

Minerva glanced out the window. Sunlit hills dotted with wildflowers rushed by in a blur outside the car windows, and the summer sky stretched out in dazzling blue. She smiled with contentment. It brought peace to believe that a loving God controlled the universe and all therein.

CHAPTER FOURTEEN

Adventures with the Youth Group

Summer 1964

"Well, here we are," said Ervin Troyer, parking the car. "I've never been to Old Man's Cave before," John Gingerich remarked, opening the door for his girlfriend Erma. "They say it's really rugged around here." Ervin, John, and Erma were all cousins to Minerva and Lovina, who rode in the backseat of the car along with Rosa Kurtz.

"I'll get your door," Ervin said to Minerva. Hurrying around to the side door, he opened it and stood back. "Are you excited?" he asked with a grin.

Minerva slid out and returned his smile. "I sure am! It's a beautiful day to tour the cave." Fleecy white clouds dappled the azure sky, and forest glades presented an alluring welcome to the youth for their day together.

The path to the cave led down a steep hill and across a swinging bridge. Lovina walked beside Minerva all the way, keeping close watch for her safety as the other girls laughed and chattered around them. Stepping off the swinging bridge, Lovina stopped and looked uncertainly at the hill before them. "Can you make it up there, Minerva?"

"Let us take her up," Ervin said from behind them. As the girls turned in surprise, he grinned and motioned to John, who had stepped up beside him. "We're at your service!"

Lovina glanced at Minerva questioningly, and she smiled. "I'm okay with it if the boys are. But I may be a heavy load!"

"As small as you are? Hah! We can carry you easily." Ervin linked his arms with John, creating a chair between them. "Lovina, will you walk beside her and hold onto her to make sure she doesn't fall?"

The hill was rugged and steep, making the trek a bit difficult for the boys. But at last they reached the top, and the youth cheered as they set Minerva down. The rest of the morning flew by, and at last they started back down the trail, heading toward the picnic area for lunch.

"Here, Minerva, sit beside me," Rosa invited, patting the seat beside her. "I'll feed you dinner, if you like."

"Thanks, Rosa." Minerva sat down at the picnic table beside her friend, watching as Rosa unpacked one of the sack lunches Mom and Lovina had prepared that morning. The girls often took turns feeding her at youth gatherings. To them it was a privilege, and even when the food missed her mouth, Minerva always just laughed along with the others.

She listened quietly now to the visiting around her, her heart thrilling to the beauty of friendship and wonders of nature that this day was unfolding. Besides the youth, there were a number of others in the park as well. Birds sang and squirrels chattered from the trees.

"Excuse me. Are you Minerva Gingerich?"

Startled, Minerva glanced up. She had noticed a group of four people standing close by, but she hadn't realized they were watching the youth. Who was this man? He looked vaguely familiar. "Yes, I'm Minerva," she said, straightening. "How do you know me?"

His eyes twinkled down at her. "I'm Dr. Donaldson."

"Oh!" She recognized him now—one of her favorite doctors from when she'd first been stricken with polio and who had helped care for her when she had had pneumonia four years ago. Excitement swept through her as she stood up. "It's good to see you again!"

"You look well," he said, smiling. "How have you been doing?"

The other youth grew quiet, listening with interest as the doctor and his former patient reminisced over years gone by. "I always knew you were a little fighter," Dr. Donaldson said with a smile when they parted. "You have a strong will to live and never give up."

The memory of that special day stayed with Minerva for the rest of her life.

"Where are those girls?" Minerva asked aloud, glancing around. Summer Bible school at Bethesda Church was in full swing, and she had attended the service this evening with three of the Kurtz sisters. But now the service was over, and the crowd was dwindling. Night had fallen and it was time to leave, but she couldn't see her friends anywhere.

The bright flash of headlights through the window caught her attention. Moving closer to the window, she recognized Rosa's little car coming up toward the church. The girls must have forgotten her. She had to laugh when the driver's door flew open and Rosa jumped out, running up the steps to the church.

"Minerva, I'm sorry! We forgot you were still here!" Rosa took her arm and led the way outside. "We're going to the drugstore tonight before we go home. I need to get a prescription, and I think we still have time to go there before it closes."

The lights inside the drugstore next to the street were already dimming by the time Rosa drove up to it and parked. "Closed," she read the sign on the door aloud. "Well, I guess we missed it this time. I'll come back again later."

As they left town, Mary asked suddenly, "Who is following us?"

The others looked back. "I saw some town boys loitering across the street," Bertha said. "When we left, they were all jumping into their vehicle. It looks like the same vehicle."

"That must be who it is," gasped Mary. "They're staying right on our trail!"

She was right. As they drove into the country, the town boys' car stayed directly behind them, slowing whenever they slowed, and speeding up whenever they did. "Go faster, Rosa!" cried Mary as they turned into another road and their shadow followed.

"I'm going as fast as this little rambler will go!" Rosa sped around a curve, glancing into the rearview mirror. "Okay, we're almost at Jonas and Emma's place. We can make it!" The car barely slowed as she whipped into the driveway. The car turned in behind them as Rosa drove on up to the porch. With great excitement, Rosa, Mary, and Bertha scrambled out of the car and made a dash for the house. From where she still sat in the backseat of the car, Minerva saw the other vehicle turn around and head in the direction it had come.

On the porch, her friends stopped suddenly. "Minerva's still out there!" Mary exclaimed.

Hurrying back down the steps, Rosa opened the door. "I'm so sorry, Minerva! We fled for safety and left you sitting in the car! How thoughtless of us!"

But Minerva was laughing. "Don't worry, Rosa. All's well that ends well!" Seeing that she wasn't upset, the others joined in her laughter as Rosa helped her up the porch steps to the house. To Minerva, the Kurtz girls were almost like sisters.

"Watch your step!"

"Don't let her fall!"

"Minerva, are you doing okay?"

"I'm fine," answered Minerva, laughing. The girls were holding her back and legs as they helped Lovina guide her up the ladder, and everyone was in good spirits. Lovina had swept out their haymow and invited friends over for a slumber party. The hay was nearly all used up, allowing the girls to spread their bedding around the loft.

Safely reaching the loft, Minerva scooted backward to sit against the wall, watching as the others came up one by one. There were ten girls in all—the Kurtz sisters, along with Susie, Fannie, and Gertie Troyer. Anna and Mary Lou Gingerich came up last, following close behind Lovina.

"I brought up a little snack," announced Lovina, placing a tray of cupcakes on the small table she'd set up. Pouring ten glasses of strawberry punch, she handed them out and sat down next to Minerva. "I hope you all like chocolate."

"Girls love chocolate, right?" Rosa asked with a grin, unwrapping her cupcake. "I should make some to offer to Mrs. Harris when we go there next week. She's such a sweet old lady."

"Last night Mrs. Harris said, 'I thought the good ol' Lord was gonna take me tonight, but I'm still here. He always supplies my needs, and even some of my wants. He brought me ice cream the other day!' " Anna laughed softly. "She's just waiting for the Lord to come and take her home."

"I always enjoy singing for those elderly people," Mary Lou commented. "It brightens my evening as much as theirs. By the way, are the youth having chorus practice this week?"

"That's what Andy said." Minerva's brother Andy was the chorus director. "He wants to teach the youth a new song," Minerva went on. " 'Near to the Heart of God' is an easy tune to learn."

"Does your family still sing together a lot?" asked Susie, reaching for her glass.

"When the married brothers and sisters come home, we do," said Lovina. "Now that Ida's gone and it's only Minerva and I left at home with our parents, we don't sing much anymore."

"Ida is such a good singer," Gertie remarked. "How is she doing since she married Cornelius?"

Minerva grinned. "She's doing well! Corny and Ida come over a lot to visit."

As twilight fell, crickets began to sing outside the open window and birds twittered softly. The girls spread out their bedding and shrouded themselves with blankets. It was a prime time for sharing deeper things of the heart.

Propping her elbows on her pillow, Esther looked expectantly at Lovina. "You're thirty-one now, right?"

Lovina nodded and glanced around the circle, her eyes twinkling. "You girls probably think I'm getting old. A lot of you are younger than I am!"

"Do you ever think about getting married?" Fannie asked.

"I know I'm getting older," Lovina said thoughtfully. "All my siblings are married now except for Minerva. I can see why you wonder if I'll ever get married and move on like they did, but . . ." Her voice trailed off, and she glanced out the window at the early stars appearing high above. "I know that Mom and Minerva need my help. I feel this is where God wants me to be."

She hesitated, and her voice softened. "Once a girl asked me if I feel I can live a fulfilled life without being married. My answer to that is yes! Besides working at home, I am free to do other things as well. When my friends asked me if I wanted to go on a western trip in '59, there was no reason why I shouldn't have. I wasn't married, and although I had a job, I could take off until I came back again."

"You went to a lot of states, didn't you?" Gertie leaned forward, her eyes shining. "I would love to go out West sometime!"

"I certainly enjoyed it," Lovina said. "We had a load of eight girls and two boys, so we took two cars. The boys drove for us. We were gone for nine weeks and went to all kinds of places." A faraway look came into her eyes. "One of the girls was a poet, and she wrote a poem about every state we went to. We visited all the states west of Indiana, as well as Canada, Mexico, and Catalina Island." She laughed. "My, was I glad to get home from that trip! Nine weeks is a long time."

Minerva remembered her own deep joy at seeing her sister return home. As the years passed by, she was beginning to depend on Lovina more and more for aid with her health issues, as well as for companionship. She didn't know what she would do without her.

CHAPTER FIFTEEN

Aunt Nervie and Aunt Vina

1965–1972

Sunbeams danced through the open window, bathing Minerva's face with warmth. She turned her head, gazing out into the morning. Birds sang merrily in the trees, and crystal drops of dew clung to the grass.

The entrance door slammed and little feet pattered into the hallway, coming toward her room. Minerva grinned and called out, "Come in here, Martha!"

"How did you know it was me?" Her five-year-old niece bounced into the room. "Miriam is here too!"

Minerva laughed. "I can always tell who you are by the sound of your footsteps."

Miriam stepped around Martha. "We wanted to help Mommi feed you this morning," she said, using the Pennsylvania Deitsh word for "Grandma." The girls were Verna's twin daughters, and they lived across the drive from Dawdi (Grandpa) and Mommi. They looked so much alike it was hard to tell them apart, especially when they wore matching colors.

Minerva saw her mom smiling as she came in behind the twins. "I need to get Minerva out of the iron lung and braid her hair first, girls. Step back, please."

The girls often liked to climb into the iron lung and lie in it while Minerva was out. The iron lung had been a part of their special "Aunt Nervie" for as long as they could remember, and they were not afraid of it. But this morning they clustered around the chair, watching intently as Mommi braided Minerva's hair and pinned on her covering.

Once in the kitchen, Miriam climbed onto Minerva's lap while Mommi prepared a bowl of cereal and mashed pills to dissolve in the milk. "All these pills Nervie has to take are so hard that she can hardly swallow them," she said to the little girls as she brought the bowl to the table. "So I usually mash them and put them in the cereal."

The twins watched Minerva closely as she began to eat. "Don't you like the pills?" Martha asked when her aunt screwed up her face.

Minerva shook her head, but her dark eyes twinkled as she went on eating. Miriam and Martha looked at each other, wide-eyed. Sometimes they complained about the food Mom made at home, but Minerva ate whatever Mommi gave her.

"Lovina is planning to do something for you girls tonight," Mommi remarked, pausing to give Minerva a drink. She smiled and lowered her voice conspiratorially. "It's for your birthday tomorrow. Can you guess what it is?"

The girls looked blank. "What does Aunt Vina do a lot when people have birthdays?" Minerva prompted.

"I know, I know! She's going to make us a cake!" Martha clapped her hands. Lovina often decorated cakes for people—weddings, farewells, or birthdays—and she especially loved to make birthday cakes for her nieces.

That evening Verna came over with her girls, where they found Lovina already in the kitchen with her cake decorating supplies laid out. Minerva sat in a chair beside her, and the girls climbed up on a bench behind the table to watch. Lovina had baked the cake in a round stainless steel bowl, and now it was sitting on the table. She smiled at the twins. "When I'm finished decorating this cake, I'll poke a hole in the center and put a little doll there. So it's going to look like a girl with a skirt!"

They crowded closer, beaming with excitement. Lovina smoothed white frosting all over the cake, then stood back to look it over. "I want to put some flowers on the skirt yet to fancy it up," she said. "What color shall I make the flowers, girls?"

"Pink! Make them pink!" they shouted.

Lovina and Minerva laughed. "All right, I'll make some pink frosting," said Lovina. Dropping a bit of red food coloring into white frosting, she mixed it until it turned a delicate shade of pink.

That was when Minerva began clicking her tongue. "What should be different?" Lovina asked, knowing that meant something didn't look right.

"It's not the right color," declared Minerva, shaking her head. "It needs to be darker!"

Lovina added a bit more coloring, then picked up her frosting bag and fastened a tip to its end. "There. It's ready now."

The twins leaned closer, watching excitedly as Lovina dotted the skirt with little star-like flowers. Last of all she mixed up yellow frosting and placed a dot in the center of each flower. Minerva watched as closely as anyone, pointing out flaws that Lovina obligingly corrected. Once she told Lovina when her sleeve was about to mess up the cake. Minerva wanted it to be perfect too. At last Lovina laid down her decorating bag, and they all stood back to admire the finished product.

"It's a pretty cake," Martha proclaimed. "Thank you, Vina, thank you!" Jumping down from the bench, she ran around the table to hug her aunt. Miriam quickly followed her. This was a birthday the twins would always remember.

"Dad, are you going to Dawdi and Mommi's?"

Noah Gingerich glanced down at his young daughter as she came running up to him. "I thought you were helping Mom in the house," he said in surprise.

Esther tossed silky strands of dark hair from her face, her eyes sparkling. "I'm all done now. Please let me hop along with you, Dad. Please, please!"

Noah chuckled. "Well, I guess you can. I'll be going right past the old home place, so we'll stop in on the way home from town and check up on Dawdi and Mommi. Here, let me help you into the car, and we're ready to go."

As they drove out the lane, Esther waved to her younger siblings and settled back in her seat like a little lady. No matter how long the errand, it was always fun to run with Dad. He whistled a tune and then burst into song. She hummed along with him, swinging her legs back and forth, reveling in the beauty of this summer day.

Noah was finished with his errand in town in record time, and soon they were rolling along the road toward Dawdi and Mommi's. "We won't be here long," Noah told his daughter as he drove into the lane. "Just a few minutes. Run on in and say hi to Mommi and Nervie."

Esther hopped out of the station wagon and ran to the front door. The aroma of freshly baked bread tingled her senses as soon as she stepped inside. She found Mommi and Aunt Nervie both in the kitchen, where Mommi was just taking a loaf of bread from the oven with Minerva sitting at the table, watching her.

Mommi turned and smiled at her. "Hi there, Esther!"

"Hi!" Esther beamed and stopped beside Minerva. "How are you today, Nervie?"

Minerva smiled down at her little niece. "I'm feeling really good. Is your dad here too?"

She nodded. "Dad had an errand to run, and I wanted to come along."

Noah came into the kitchen. "Smells good in here," he boomed.

"We'll send a loaf or two home with you," Mommi said, smiling. Esther's mouth watered. She could hardly wait to eat a piece of Mommi's delicious soft bread!

When they left minutes later, Esther waved to her aunt, who stood in the doorway, her body gently rocking from side to side with each breath she took. She was smiling a see-you-again-soon smile, and shook what little goodbye her hand could muster. The sweet parting sent warm circles around Esther's heart as the car turned onto the road.

"Nervie, tell me a dory. Pwease?" Clutching a doll in one hand, little Veronica tapped Minerva's knee with the other. Veronica now lived across the drive from her grandparents, having moved there after her cousins Miriam and Martha moved to a different house. She often begged her mother for permission to come across the drive to Dawdi and Mommi's.

"I'll tell you a story about your aunt Vina," Minerva said, leaning forward. "Long, long ago when Lovina was just a tiny baby, Mommi took her out in the yard and put her on a blanket to play. We had some chickens, and they came up to look at this baby, clucking and walking all around her. Mommi went on to the barn to milk the cows, where she opened a gate to let them in. There were some frisky calves that slipped out with the cows. They ran right toward the chickens and that baby, and jumped over everything."

Veronica listened, her eyes wide as Minerva went on.

"Mommi's heart was in her throat. She raced toward those chickens as they ran and clucked, and she grabbed her baby and whisked her into the house." Minerva paused and smiled. "The Lord saved Lovina that day, Veronica. He took care of her, and He takes care of us too."

Veronica held up the doll in her arms. "Will God take care of my dolly?"

Minerva laughed softly. "I'm sure He will if you ask Him to." She watched Veronica fondly as the four-year-old ran off to the next room. She loved when her nieces and nephews came to visit, and found joy in how unique and special each one was.

Miriam and Martha were spending the day at their grandparents' house. After playing in the yard awhile, they ran over to the porch, where Lovina and Minerva were sitting. "We were picking flowers, and we wanted to bring some to you," Miriam said, handing a bouquet to Lovina. "Vina, could you arrange these for me?" She knew her aunt Lovina loved creating dried flower bouquets. Sometimes her mother and aunts came to Mommi's for a "dried flower day," bringing their own flowers along. Lovina always showed them how to arrange the bouquets just so.

Now Lovina turned Miriam's flowers over in her hands. "Sure! These daisies should go right here . . . and this sunflower in the middle . . . then this spray of ferns right here on the left side. Snip the stems a bit shorter—and there you are!" She smiled and handed it back to Miriam.

Miriam looked at the bouquet from all angles and beamed with satisfaction. "It's pretty. You make good bouquets!"

CHAPTER SIXTEEN

A Full Life

To my dear, special sister, Minerva Gingerich,

My heart has been blessed to have such a sister as you. You have so cheerfully and willingly accepted the lot in life that God has chosen for you. Many times it has been a great lesson for me.

On August 1, 1972, it was twenty years since you were taken to the hospital with that dreaded disease: polio. You were thirteen years old at the time. I can well remember the time they left home with you for the hospital, not fully realizing how ill you actually were. You were placed in an iron lung where, for many days after, your life hung on a mere thread. One thing was sure: the Lord had a purpose in letting you remain with us.

You were put in isolation and you could not swallow anything for approximately three weeks. They fed you intravenously till you could swallow again. Your ability to swallow came back very slowly.

Fannie's pen flew across the page, pouring out memories from those days so long ago. More than once, the words blurred as tears misted her eyes, and she had to stop to brush them away.

. . . This iron lung, which today stands in your bedroom, is a monument to each of us—your brothers, sisters, nieces, nephews, and friends. It is a symbol of the method God is using to preserve your life. Children who are not acquainted with an iron lung may be afraid of it, but it is not so with your nieces and nephews. They would rather play in it. Sometimes they beg to be put into it to demonstrate to visitors how it works. To us it spells love and peace, for it makes us think of this special sister and aunt, who is a blessing to us all and has a special place in our hearts.

In the wintertime you and I would agree that it would be nice to be in Florida since we, and especially you, are so susceptible to colds, sore throat, and pneumonia. We try to accept the fact that we cannot go. But we comfort ourselves with the thought that warm weather will come again.

I can just see you on one of those nice spring mornings. You would like to go outside, so you walk to the door. Your arms hang limply by your side. You cannot lift your hand to turn the knob. I can hear you call out, "Mom, come open the door!"

In the summertime it's common to see you sitting out in the sun, soaking up the warm sunshine. If one of those pesky flies sits on your nose, you either try to blow it off or shake your head, because you cannot lift your hands to shoo it away. If you have an itchy spot, you say, "Oh, hurry and scratch me," and we gladly scratch away! We are thankful the Lord gave you the strength to walk so freely.

Well, it's time for bed again. As I think of how easy it is for me to slip into bed, my mind goes to your bedroom. I can see Mom tucking you into the iron lung. She is trying to make the foam collar airtight so you will get the right amount of suction and pressure in the iron lung. She covers you up—a little tug here, a little tug there, and finally she has you comfortable. She has worked about one hour now. The switch is flipped on and the iron lung takes over the work of keeping your breathing going. Now you can relax your lung and neck muscles and fall into a peaceful sleep.

Good night, my dear, special sister. After thinking of all you have endured and knowing you still have a deep trust and faith in God, you can understand why I call you "special." God bless you.

With a prayer in her heart, Fannie folded up the pages and placed them in an envelope. Next, she reached for a poem that had been placed on Minerva's iron lung at the hospital. Smiling, she read the words again.

My Friend Was There

I'm isolated, flat in bed;
None can come in is what they said.
But He came in, was there each day;
They could not keep my Friend away.
All other ones stood by the door;
They could not pass the threshold o'er,
But He came in—He had no fear;
I felt His presence always near.
In the early morning, noon or night,
My room was radiant with His light,
Yes, He was there—came in each day;
They could not keep my Friend away.
I saw Him in the doctor's care,
And in the white-robed nurses there;
In those who helped my ills to mend,
I felt the presence of my Friend.

Fannie placed the poem in the envelope as well. She planned to send it to Pathway Publishers for publication in *Family Life*, under "A Page for Shut-Ins."[1]

"Come in, come in!" Dawdi's kindly face beamed as he met Noah and Fannie's family at the door, welcoming them in from

[1] The full article was published in the *Family Life*, November 1972.

the chilly autumn evening. "Give Mommi your wraps and come sit in the living room."

Esther handed her coat and shawl to Mommi and then hurried to the little card table where Minerva was reading the *Budget.* The pages were spread out before her, and her reading glasses were perched on the end of her nose. She grinned at Esther and her sisters as they crowded around. "So you came to see us again?"

"What's the news in *Budget* land?" Esther's oldest sister Ruth asked.

Lowering her head, Minerva turned a page with her mouth. "Look at this article here, Ruth. One of your friends just went on a mission trip overseas."

"Really?" Ruth stepped closer. "It's amazing how much you find out, Nervie. You know the people of *Budget* land better than most of us do!"

They laughed together, and Minerva said, "I just have more time than others to read and digest it."

Esther wandered toward the bookcase, where Dawdi and Mommi kept all kinds of little books for children. She was deep in a story when she heard Minerva say, "Don't you think it's time for popcorn, Lovina?"

Lovina stood up. "I'll have it ready soon. Do some of you girls want to help me?"

In the kitchen, Esther stood beside her aunt, watching her stir a pitcher of bright red punch. "Hand me those cups one by one, Esther, and I'll fill them," Lovina told her. "Then we'll pass them out, along with popcorn and ice cream."

Esther gave a happy little skip as she took a plate of popcorn to the living room. It was always such fun to come to Dawdi's.

"Nervie!"

The call floated on the breeze toward Minerva, where she sat on the grass watching Mom work in the garden. In minutes, six of her young nieces burst around the corner. "Want to go on a walk with us?" Lillian asked. "We need to get some eggs at the neighbors'."

"Sure, I'll go with you!" Minerva smiled and stood up. The summer day was mellow and golden, with clear blue skies, and flowers blowing in the wind. It was perfect for a walk.

"You can hold the basket if you want to, Nervie." Lillian's sister Delilah carefully placed the handle of the basket over her arm, and they started off.

On the highway that passed by the house, vehicles occasionally rushed by. "Look at that!" Becky exclaimed suddenly. "A butterfly flew against that car, and now it's lying beside the road." She hurried toward the butterfly and picked it up. "It's dead, but it's pretty!"

"It looks like a monarch butterfly," Lillian commented.

Becky's eyes shone as she studied the delicate creature. "I'm going to take this to Lovina," she declared. "She always uses the dead butterflies we bring for her projects."

"Lovina is always doing something," Veronica remarked. "Becky and I were over last Sunday afternoon for a while and watched her put together a scrapbook sheet. She often does that on Sunday."

The girls chattered on as they walked in the neighbors' lane. The eggs were quickly gathered and they started back to Dawdi's, with Minerva still holding the egg basket. But by now she was feeling tired, and her steps began to lag, causing her to drop behind the others. Her nieces, chattering and laughing as they stopped here and there to pick flowers, did not notice. When they began pulling ahead, Minerva called, "Hey, girls, slow down! I can't carry these eggs anymore."

Startled, the girls turned around. As they saw the tears in Minerva's eyes, they came running back. "I'm so sorry, Minerva," Delilah said, taking the basket. "I should have noticed that you couldn't keep up anymore. We'll walk with you from now on." Not for the world would she intentionally hurt Minerva! They all loved to spend time with this special aunt.

Christmas was coming. Pure white snow covered the ground, and many people were lighting up their house windows with candles.

In the Gingerich home, the children crowded around the table, watching their aunt Lovina make new candles for their own windows. Over the years, Minerva had received lots of candles as gifts, and Lovina had saved every one of them. Now she had brought out some of those old candles to create new ones.

First she melted the candles. Then she poured the wax into molds of all shapes and sizes. Next she put a wick in each one and waited for it to harden. At last a brand new candle stood before them, with a new size, shape, and color.

"What do you think?" Lovina asked, turning to her nieces and nephews with a twinkle in her eyes. "Are some of these nice enough to give away as gifts?"

Their cheers were answer enough. No matter what project she was busy with—working in the garden or painting pictures on the smooth, flat stones they brought to her—Lovina was always doing something, with Minerva right beside her to watch. The two were a team, and it was always fun to be around them.

CHAPTER SEVENTEEN

Dad

1974

Minerva sat next to Lovina at the table, watching her sister put the finishing touches on an oil painting. "It looks good, Lovina," she said, leaning closer.

Laying aside her brush, Lovina studied the painting critically. It featured folded hands lifted in prayer. "This is all I'm going to do for one day," she said. "It'll soon be time to go home."

Minerva glanced around the table at the other class members. Lovina had decided to join a group of girls in taking art classes at Marysville High School, and Minerva was allowed to go along. It was always a highlight of her day.

Her eyes shadowed as her thoughts turned toward home. Now thirty-five, Minerva could see how her parents were aging. Long ago, various people had told them, "Something is wrong with your dad." They hadn't wanted to believe it, but in recent years it had become evident that something was indeed wrong. Dad had finally been diagnosed with Parkinson's disease, suffering from the illness for nearly eleven years now. He was on medication, and they had oxygen tanks at home in case he ever needed them.

Minerva was thankful that her mother still seemed to be doing well. Whether it was cooking, gardening, or cleaning, Emma worked hard. And she was an excellent nurse, caring lovingly for Minerva's needs.

"Are you coming, Minerva?" Lovina's voice broke through her thoughts, and Minerva looked up to see her sister smiling down at her. She smiled back and stood up. "I'm coming."

When they arrived home, their parents were sitting together on the porch swing, rocking slowly back and forth. "How was your evening?" Dad asked.

"I enjoyed it a lot," Lovina answered, sitting down on the porch step. "I'm always learning new techniques in oil painting."

"If you keep on the way you are, you'll be doing really good work," said Minerva.

"Someday I'd like to do a painting of mountains and a blue sky," Lovina said, her eyes lighting up. "When I went out West, I saw some magnificent sights. I wish I would have had a way to paint some of them right there."

Silence fell, broken only by the creak of the swing. Then Minerva turned to Dad. "Did you get things done in your shop today?"

"A little," answered Dad. "But I was thinking I'd go out and watch Ora's boys tomorrow. They're planning to work in the field."

As crickets began to sing and stars appeared, contentment stole over Minerva's heart. She couldn't think of any place she'd rather be than here at home with her parents and older sister. They had good times together.

Jonas walked toward the pasture, his gait slow and shuffling. His once-black hair was gray now, and the Parkinson's disease had taken its toll, causing tremors throughout his whole body. They stopped only when he slept.

Such a crippling illness made one realize the brevity of life. As he walked toward the field, Jonas pondered the years that lay behind him. He seemed to see again the young boy, weeping at the grave that had laid both his parents to rest. He relived the years he'd spent with his half-brother before coming back to Ohio as a youth. So many memories, all a part of what had shaped his life and who he had become.

Then had come the crowning of his manhood: a time filled with fragrant dreams and love as he joined hands with the sweet young lady who'd promised to be his wife. Their commitment to each other had deepened throughout the years, strengthening their love as they shared the joys and trials of life. Jonas smiled as he reached the barbed wire fence that bordered the pasture. God had richly blessed him.

He stood still for a moment, watching his grandsons working in the field. Ora had bought the farm, and his sons—Mark, Paul, Marvin, and Samuel—were all out there. Jonas glanced toward the space under the barbed wire. It was easily high enough to crawl under and go into the field.

Getting down on his hands and knees, he tried to move forward. But his body wouldn't cooperate. With growing alarm, Jonas tried to stand up again, but he couldn't move. Minutes crept by as he struggled on alone, growing weaker and weaker. At last he gave up, too exhausted to keep trying, and began calling for help.

From where Samuel was walking toward the barn, he heard the faint call. Straightening, he listened more closely. There was the voice again—someone pleading for help. And it sounded like Dawdi!

Samuel caught his breath. Breaking into a run, he dashed around the corner of the barn. Dawdi was lying under the fence, unable to get up, his face lined with exhaustion and sweat.

Stopping just long enough to assure his grandfather that he would get help, Samuel rushed to the field toward his brothers. "Dawdi is lying under the fence and he can't move!" he cried.

The brothers wasted no time. Quickly placing their grandpa in a wagon, they took him to the house and put him to bed. There Emma hooked him up to oxygen, following instructions that the doctor had given them a month earlier. With his body getting the air it needed, Jonas was able to rest.

Minerva stood long at her dad's bedside that night, watching him sleep. In the dim lighting he looked peaceful, the shadows across his face hiding the lines that age had marked there. It hurt to see him lying there in pain. He had been her strong, loving father ever since she could remember, doing his best to care for her. She depended on him so much.

"Minerva?" Emma spoke in a whisper as she touched her arm. "It's time for bed."

Minerva nodded and glanced back at the bed one last time. "Good night, Dad," she said softly.

"Be good today, Dad," said Lovina with a grin, pausing at the door.

From where he sat at the table with a bowl of cereal, Jonas glanced up and smiled. "Off to work again?"

"It's my job, you know," she responded lightly. "I'll be back again this evening to see you." Waving at Mom and Minerva, who were both sitting at the table with Dad, she stepped out the door.

In the past two weeks, Jonas's condition had improved. Lovina found herself humming as she walked out to meet Ina Troyer, who had stopped in to pick her up for work. The spring morning teemed with freshness and life, relaxing her spirit.

Her morning at the bookstore passed quickly, with customers drifting in and out. Lovina welcomed each one with a smile and a cheery greeting that brightened many faces. "God bless you, Lovina," one elderly lady said as she took her bag of purchases and turned to leave. "We need cheerful workers like you."

I love my job here at the store, Lovina mused as she watched the lady leave the store. *I can't think of anything else I'd rather do.*

Behind her the telephone rang, jarring her from her reverie. She answered it on the second ring. "Hello?"

"Lovina," her mom's voice came urgently across the line. "Dad had a heart attack, and we're taking him to the hospital. I wanted to let you know. We'll be coming down Main Street in the squad, and we'll pass where you're working."

Lovina's mind raced as the meaning of Mom's words sank in. "Will you stop in and pick me up?" she asked quickly. "I want to go along."

"We'll be there soon," came the answer.

In minutes the squad stopped by just long enough for Lovina to climb in. On the way, Mom explained what had happened. "Dad overworked himself this morning when he tried to walk to the bathroom. The effort was too much for him."

Minerva, Fannie, and Verna met them at the hospital in Marysville. Ida, at home with three preschoolers and a new baby, wasn't able to come until later. That day was a long one. Minerva stood at her dad's bedside in the ICU, watching his pale face. He was hooked up to IVs, with a monitor showing his heartbeat. It was clear that his strength was quickly ebbing away.

"Dad told me today that he doesn't have anything against anyone," Lovina shared that evening as the family sat together in the lobby. "I believe he's ready to go if the Lord calls him home."

"He also told us to take good care of the grandchildren,"

Noah added, his voice husky with emotion. "He's concerned about their spiritual needs."

Tears came to Minerva's eyes. What a blessing to know that Dad was at peace with God. His physical strength might be leaving him, but he was spiritually strong, firmly grounded in the faith and love of his Saviour.

Thinking that Dad was in stable condition, the family traveled home that evening with plans to return the next day. But as bedtime neared, a call came from the hospital. "Your father is getting low. If you want to see him again, you need to come."

Ora and Noah were the only ones in the room with Dad when he took his last breath. As the lines traveling up and down on the monitor became a straight line, his spirit was carried away to glory. With tears in their eyes, the two oldest sons left the bedside to call the rest of the family.

The funeral was held in the new shop that Ora had built. A balmy day greeted the people who came to gather in the shop around the family. Others were seated in the farmhouse, where another sermon was preached for those gathered there.

Nearly seven hundred people gathered outside in the cemetery for the graveside service. As she watched the pallbearers lower the coffin into the ground, Minerva remembered how one doctor had said, "Jonas passed on so easily; he was relaxed." Dad had been seventy years old when he passed away. Now they were able to believe he was in heaven, fully healed from his suffering and living with his Lord forever. While she took comfort in this, her heart grieved for the hole left in their family. How they would miss him!

Life without their father was a difficult adjustment for all of them. Mom, Lovina, and Minerva were the only ones left at home now. With Lovina working away from home, there were often only two people in the house. The table seemed too empty at mealtimes. Evenings lacked Dad's stable presence. Now that her father was gone, Minerva realized just how much she had depended on him.

She knew the others felt the loss as well. Dad was no longer there when her brothers and sisters stopped in. Dawdi wasn't there to play with his grandchildren when they came to visit. When they sang together, his voice was greatly missed.

But they found that life had a way of going on, easing the pain and bringing joy to their lives again. Lovina started a new job at Miller's Gospel Books in Plain City where, besides selling books, she also imprinted Bibles for people. Bethesda Church had become involved in a ministry for the inmates at the London, Ohio, prison, where they handed out Bible courses from Lamp & Light Publishers.

"If the inmates fill out their courses correctly, they are rewarded with a free study Bible," Lovina said as she relaxed with Mom and Minerva on the porch one evening at sunset. "Often they want their names imprinted on the Bible." She hesitated and then added softly, "When I go to work in the morning, I pray that I can be a witness for God. If even one person is changed by receiving a Bible, it'll be worth it."

"Do you enjoy working at the store?" Minerva asked.

Lovina smiled. "I certainly do. Some days are rather stressful, but it's rewarding." A thoughtful look came into her eyes. "You know, there's nowhere I'd rather be than here at home with you and Mom, and working at the store. I feel that this is where God wants me to be." She glanced toward the lawn, vacant now of the nieces and nephews who often played there, and smiled. "He has blessed me with a full life."

As Lovina fell silent, Minerva looked out over the lawn, almost able to see little children running in the grass. God had blessed her life too. For many years now He had granted her good health, and she was thankful for that. Lately, however, she had not been sleeping well at night. She wondered if something was wrong. But she knew that God was with her, and that was enough to give her peace.

CHAPTER EIGHTEEN

Travels
1975–1977

"Is this the right place?" Noah asked as he steered his car into the parking lot.

Mom checked the map. "It looks like it." She glanced back at Minerva and smiled. "Are you ready for this?"

Minerva smiled back. "Oh, yes!" She had looked forward to this handicap reunion in Holmes County for weeks.

Getting out of the car, Noah came around to help her out. "Now be careful and have fun! I'll see you both in a couple hours."

"Thanks, Noah." Emma took Minerva's arm and led her up the walk to the house. A smiling lady met them at the door, taking their wraps and ushering them inside. "Make sure you get name tags at that table over there," she said, indicating a table nearby. "There will be an introduction and a little program later."

As Minerva followed her mother toward the table, she glanced around. The gathering was rather small—around fifty people— but all were smiling and visiting together. There were some people in wheelchairs, and others with walkers and canes.

"Here, Minerva," Mom said, turning toward her. "I'll put this name tag on your dress."

When at last they went to sit down for the program, Minerva

found herself sitting beside a lady her own age. "My name is Fannie Beachy," the lady introduced herself. "I've been blind all my life. I went to a blind school in Columbus until I was through eighth grade. Over the years I've learned lots of things—like cooking and sewing, which comes in handy since I live by myself." She smiled. "I also have my own Braille Bible, and an accordion and guitar that I often play."

Minerva looked at the Amish lady with amazement. "You know how to do all that?"

Fannie laughed. "Well, it took years to get to this place! Remember, I went to a blind school. It took time and effort to learn, but I never gave up. I wanted to do all I could for myself."

"Nothing gets you down, does it?"

"Life only gets you down if you let it," Fannie answered with spirit. "God gives strength for each new day! He asks us only to live for Him and be happy."

There was no time for further visiting as the program began, but Minerva thought often about her new friend's words as the day passed by. As she saw the various handicaps that afflicted the people around her, she thanked God anew for what He had done for her. Fannie was right—true peace lay in accepting God's will, whatever it was, and being happy with it.

That first meeting was the beginning of a lifelong friendship. Fannie stopped in several times after that to visit the Gingerich ladies, and they liked to call her for her birthday. Fannie was an inspiration to all of them.

"I have an idea," Emma announced, a smile playing around her lips.

At the card table, Minerva glanced up from the letter she was writing with a typewriter. The pencil in her mouth enabled her to press the keys, and she could watch its progress on the paper. Now she sat back. "What is it, Mom?"

Mom was smiling over the blocks she was cutting for a comforter—a project she often did for people. Lovina sat on the couch nearby, reading a story to the children clustered around her. Noah and Fannie had come by earlier that evening, leaving their children with Mommi while they went to town.

Lovina glanced up from the book. "Yes, Mom, what is your idea?"

Mom's eyes twinkled as she set her scissors aside. "What would you girls say about going to Florida?"

"Florida?" Lovina nearly dropped the book in her surprise. "Are you serious?"

Mom nodded, her excitement evident. "Lester and Sarah have been asking us to come, and I think now would be as good a time as any." On his return from Belize to the States, Lester had been asked to serve as bishop at Sunnyside Church in Florida. So once again they had said goodbye to their family and moved to the southern state close to the ocean.

"And Sarah's mom and her sister Bertha are down there right now, so we could visit them too," Lovina realized. "I think we should go!"

Minerva agreed wholeheartedly. She hadn't taken such a trip for many years. "How long would we be there?" she asked.

"Enough to make it worthwhile," Mom declared. "I thought maybe nine weeks."

"Nine weeks?" Minerva sat up straighter. "I don't want to start off for Florida until I know there's an iron lung in place for me down there!"

Before Mom could answer, the door opened, letting in a cold gust of wind as Noah and Fannie stepped inside. "My, it's nice and warm in here," exclaimed Noah. He swept up a small boy who had come running and tossed him into the air. "What have you youngsters been up to? Did you behave?"

"For the most part," Lovina said, glancing sideways at Minerva. Her younger sister had her own method of punishment for her nieces and nephews—using her foot to spank them when they didn't behave.

Minerva's eyes twinkled back at Lovina. "They all wanted to check out my iron lung again," she said casually to Noah. "Some children are afraid of it, but not them! I guess they're all used to it."

Fannie smiled and sat down on the sofa. "It's a part of their lives. So how have you all been doing?"

"It certainly helped out when Noah repaired the basement last week," Mom said. "There hasn't been any water down there since then."

Noah grinned and sat down beside Fannie. "Well, I'm glad to help out in any way I can."

Mom leaned forward. "There's something I'd like to ask you about, Noah. The girls and I are thinking about taking a trip to Florida to visit Lester and Sarah, but Minerva doesn't want to go until she knows that she'll have an iron lung."

"We'll take care of it," Noah said instantly. "You need to get away sometimes."

"Perhaps this would be a good time to visit our niece Emma in El Salvador," Lovina remarked. "I've been wanting to visit her for a long time now."

As the night deepened, Noah and Fannie gathered their children and left. Minerva stood at the door for a moment, watching the car lights until they faded in the distance. Stars appeared in the sky, and the night creatures' choir filled the air. Behind her, Lovina softly began to sing their favorite song,

"No Tears in Heaven."

The beautiful words blended with the peace and calm of the night. Minerva looked up into the starry heavens and thought of how she'd once heard a minister preach about the plan of salvation. "We need to be excited," he had said emphatically. "When God calls us home, we will be made perfect!"

Perfect. It was hard to imagine, but she knew that day was approaching. With all her heart, she wanted to be ready when the Lord called her home.

The ocean waved in aqua swells and crested with white foam as Uncle Andy steered his boat from the bay. "This is the Gulf of Mexico," he announced. "Mary and I often come out here."

Lifting her face toward the sun, Minerva laughed aloud. "I think I need to buy a beach house to live in during the winter like you and Mary, Uncle Andy. It's beautiful out here!"

"It's hard to believe that Florida has eighty-degree weather in February," Mom agreed. Adjusting her hat, she leaned back against the side of the boat. "This is really relaxing."

"I was so excited when I heard you were coming down here to visit," Bertha said to Minerva. "It's even more fun to visit my sister's family when more people from home show up too!"

Minerva smiled. This trip was turning out to be one of the most exciting experiences in her life. She was thankful first of all to Noah, who had lived up to his word in providing an iron lung for her in Florida. He had picked up a U-Haul, rented a machine from an iron lung center in Augusta, Georgia, and then took it on down to Lester and Sarah's.

"It's all ready for you," Noah had said when he called Minerva. With the iron lung taken care of, she was able to relax and enjoy her trip. It was now six weeks since they had flown to Florida. After the first two weeks, Lovina had flown to El Salvador to visit Emma, but Mom, Bertha, and Bertha's mother Lizzie Ann Kurtz had been with her the whole time.

"I love spending time with my brother's family," Minerva said now. "Their little boys are so sweet!"

"I'm thankful that your health is good enough for you to take this trip, Minerva," Lizzie Ann said, joining the conversation. "At one time you wouldn't have been able to."

At one time. As though a cloud had passed over the sun, Minerva's thoughts took an ominous turn. Even here with her brother's family, she couldn't sleep well at night. Lizzie Ann was right—at one time she wouldn't have been able to take a trip like this. Would her health continue its downward progress and send her to the hospital again?

But as she gazed up into the peaceful blue sky, Minerva felt her tension melt away. Life was beautiful right now, and she wouldn't spoil it by worrying about her future. That was in God's hands.

CHAPTER NINETEEN

Tracheotomy

January–February 1980

"Does this make you feel better?" Lovina stood beside Minerva's iron lung, doing her best to make her sister feel comfortable. Each time, Minerva shook her head and voiced another discomfort. As the long night wore on, Lovina grew desperate.

"I think it's time to do something," she said to Mom the next morning. "Minerva didn't sleep at all last night. She's complaining of stinging in her feet too."

Mom studied her daughter's pale face with concern. "You've slept a total of eight hours this week, Minerva. I'm going to call the doctor."

After Dr. Carr examined Minerva thoroughly, he stated, "Her tongue muscles are becoming weak and deteriorated. When she lies in the iron lung, her tongue muscles slide back on the windpipe and cut off the air. This makes her wake up. How long has this been going on?"

"She hasn't been sleeping well for a couple years now," Mom said. "But lately it's been getting worse."

Meeting her gaze, Dr. Carr spoke kindly. "Your daughter will have to go to the hospital, Mrs. Gingerich. They have several respirators there and will provide something to help her."

Minerva was admitted to the hospital on January 23 and placed in Room 341. While her mom and sisters waited in the lobby, the doctors took Minerva away for examination. *She had tests and X-rays,* Ida wrote in her diary. *Lovina stayed with Minerva while the rest of us went home. Still uncomfortable. No sleep all night.*

"I feel anxious," Minerva said quietly when the others left the room. "Lovina, will you pray with me tonight?"

Lovina moved closer, reaching out to place a hand on her head. "Of course I will." All through the long night, she stood beside the iron lung, praying with Minerva. By the time morning dawned, a measure of peace had settled over Minerva's heart, and she felt ready for whatever lay ahead.

On the second day, Ida wrote, *Minerva still had no sleep during the day. Very uncomfortable, at times in misery. Doctors started coming in to check her. Found nothing unusual, but thought her tongue muscles are weakening. Possibility for tracheotomy.*

The doctors had never worked with this kind of illness before. They began experimenting on Minerva with various treatments, such as placing tubes in her mouth to clamp her tongue forward. It made her gag. Next they put a rubber tube through her nose and down her throat. Nothing helped.

By Friday, the family realized that a tracheotomy was likely the only option they had of restoring Minerva's health. She was declining, and it was imperative that they do something. Still, it came as a surprise when two doctors suddenly entered the room, medical bags in hand. "We've come to perform the tracheotomy," one of them announced without warning, walking toward Minerva's bed.

The news felt sudden. Weren't they going to try a few other things first? "One of my doctors recently started a new experiment on me," Minerva said hesitantly. After a few moments of conversation, the surgeons realized their patient was not ready to consent to surgery, and they packed up their bags to leave.

As the door closed behind them, Minerva's constant care nurse, Mary Greenlee, spoke up. "Wouldn't you be ready to have the tracheotomy performed, Minerva?" She glanced at the family sitting around the room, including them in her question. "This is your last chance. If you don't do it now, you'll have to go all through the weekend like this."

And I don't think you'll make it through another weekend. Though the nurse didn't say it, the words hung silently in midair. Emma took a deep breath and spoke for all of them. "Yes, we would like to have it done, Mary."

Quickly leaving the room, Mary hurried down the hall and turned the corner. The doctors were far ahead by now. Breaking into a run, she dashed through the corridor after them. "They want to do the surgery after all," she called breathlessly as she drew near.

Once again, Dr. Semm and Dr. Richardson returned to Minerva's room and unpacked their bags. Emma and Lovina stayed in the room, watching as the doctors began the operation. Numbing Minerva's throat, they began cutting through the skin to expose the trachea, explaining the process the whole time. "The windpipe in your throat is the trachea," said Dr. Semm. "The hole is called a stoma."

When the doctors were finished, Minerva began hyperventilating, unable to get a true breath as air flowed rapidly in and out of the opening in her throat. "Minerva!" Dr. Richardson called, bending over her. "You have to stop! Slow down, slow down!" But she had no control over her breathing. Quickly the doctors stitched around the hole and lifted her up, but that did not help.

Dr. Richardson barked an order, and in minutes other doctors were rushing into the room. "Get a respirator for this patient immediately," Dr. Richardson commanded. While they hurried to do his bidding, he turned back to Minerva. "We're going to fit a trach tube into your stoma," he told her. "The ventilator will hook up to it and allow you to breathe."

From where she stood by the door, Lovina watched as he tried to fit a tracheostomy tube into the hole in Minerva's throat. "Size four is too small; it doesn't give her enough air," Dr. Richardson said at length, glancing toward Dr. Semm. "Make the hole a little bigger, and I'll try size six."

That first trach made her bleed! Lovina felt lightheaded as she caught sight of the red stains on the narrow tube that Dr. Richardson was setting aside. This whole situation was becoming too much for her to handle. Turning quickly, she hurried to the restroom nearby and lay down on the floor, trying to fight off her weakness.

The doctors found a ventilator on another floor and brought it to Minerva's room. With this machine, they were able to stabilize their patient. As she lay still, concentrating on breathing normally, Minerva overheard one doctor say, "We got her just in time." She knew then that the danger was past, and God had spared her life once again.

The sun set that evening in a fiery splendor of color and wind. Minerva watched through the hospital window, marveling at the beauty. She felt more relaxed than she had in a long time. The time had come to say goodbye to the iron lung; the ventilator, hooked up to the tracheostomy tube, took its place. Although it was an adjustment, the ventilator did a good job of breathing for her and providing the air she desperately needed for her body.

From where he was writing on his chart, Dr. Bhandari glanced up and smiled at her. "Are you still doing okay, Minerva?"

She nodded and watched as he bent over his chart again. He

had stayed with her all afternoon as she adjusted to the ventilator, making sure she remained in stable condition. What a blessing to have doctors who cared about her and did the best they could for her. God truly worked miracles through them.

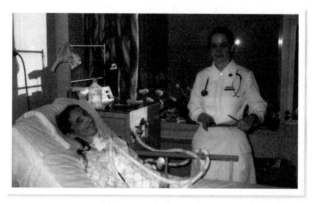

Minerva with the tracheostomy tube inserted.

CHAPTER TWENTY

Burdens

February 1980

It was midnight. Rain slashed against the hospital windows as the wind rose, howling with a lonely sound that made Minerva shudder. If only she could sleep!

Does God really love you? The taunting whisper seemed to ride on the night winds. *He's taken away the use of your hands. Is He going to take your voice now too? How will you be able to communicate?* One of the results of the surgery was that Minerva could no longer speak aloud unless the hole in her throat was covered by the respirator or by someone's finger. Even when she was hooked up to the respirator, she had to wait for it to give her breaths so she could speak. Because of that, she could only say a few words at a time, with a pause between phrases.

Tears came to her eyes. "How will I cope?" she whispered, staring into the darkness. "How will people be able to understand me when I can't talk out loud if I'm not on my respirator? Oh, God, I need help! Give me the patience I need to work through this!"

Did God even hear her prayer? Tonight He seemed far away. The darkness deepened, closing around her heart with a weight so intense it was like a physical burden. She struggled in its bonds, growing weaker and weaker. She couldn't handle this alone.

Oh, God, give me patience! Her heart's cry winged its way heavenward, reaching the throne of grace. *Help me to truly believe the Bible verse I read tonight—that when I call unto you, you will answer me, and show me great and mighty things, which I know not. Give me patience.*

Night was still upon the land, but the oppression of her soul had lifted to heaven's glorious light. Peace stole into Minerva's heart as she continued to commune with her heavenly Father, surrendering her life into His hands. Blessed sleep overtook her just as the first rays of dawn were streaking the sky.

During the second week of her stay in the hospital, Minerva shared her desire to be anointed. "I want to ask the Lord to heal me if it's His will," she said to her mother. "But if not . . ." She hesitated. "I want to be able to accept whatever He sends."

Emma looked at her with sympathy. "Has it been hard for you, Minnie?"

Minerva's dark eyes misted with tears. "I've been praying every day for patience," she said quietly. "I pray for it over and over again. It's so hard . . ." Her voice caught on a sob. Mom placed an arm around her shoulders and cried with her.

"We must keep trusting the Lord, Minerva," Mom said finally. "He has a purpose in this."

"I keep reminding myself of a verse I read in Jeremiah recently," Minerva said, looking at her mother. "It says, 'Call unto me, and I will answer thee, and shew thee great and mighty things, which thou knowest not.' I want to be at peace with God, willing to accept whatever He chooses to do with my life. If this is how I can serve Him, I'll accept it." She bowed her head. "May His will be done."

The sun shone brightly on the city of Columbus. Traffic rushed past the towering walls of the hospital, unmindful of the crisis brewing within.

On the third floor of the hospital, a nurse rushed down the hallway, anxious to find the doctors. The patient in Room 341 was hyperventilating and shaking violently all over, which were signs of a severe fever. Already the fever had spiked to 102.8 degrees, and Minerva was complaining of a headache. The nurse explained all this hurriedly to Dr. Wyatt and Dr. Waggoner as she led the way back down the hall.

Blood tests revealed that Minerva had developed four lung infections—pneumonia, strep throat, staph, and Haemophilus influenza. They put her on IVs for the night, and for a couple days after that she was quarantined. Her door was closed at all times, and any person who entered had to wear a gown and mask. Though it was discouraging, Minerva remembered that special promise: "Call unto me, and I will answer thee . . ." God had a reason for her illness, and He was working for her good. In this she found comfort and the courage to go on.

"Minerva? You have visitors." Opening the door, Lovina stood back to let them enter.

Glancing up, Minerva smiled a welcome. All the Kurtz sisters were married now, and Rosa had moved away. But Mary and Bertha had come to visit her with their husbands, bringing gifts and cheer to the room.

"My sister Esther has pneumonia right now and couldn't come with us," Mary said, sitting down on a chair beside Minerva's bed.

"People were coming into the hospital with pneumonia last week," said Lovina, joining them. "The nurses said, 'Let's get Minerva out of here,' but then she came down with four lung infections. She's doing better now, though," she added, smiling at Minerva. "One day last week, one of the doctors was nearly at his wit's end. They were trying all kinds of antibiotics, but she just wasn't getting better. Finally I asked the doctors, 'Couldn't we try to put Vicks vapor rub on her chest?' He knew of nothing else to do, so he agreed. He made the comment that this is something his grandma used to do. I guess we were using some old-fashioned remedies!"

Minerva lay quietly as the conversation flowed around her. Many friends had come in to visit her since she'd been in the hospital. She appreciated their encouragement, but she struggled with accepting her inability to speak. Sometimes people asked her a question, and she would try to mouth her reply. But instead of watching her lips, they tried to listen and when they nodded as though they understood, she knew they really didn't. As a result, she was learning to keep her words limited with people who weren't used to lip reading, but it was still a little frustrating.

Dismissing the thoughts, Minerva focused on what the others were saying. But when her visitors left, the enemy bombarded her once again with discouragement. Was it going to be like this all her life when she tried to communicate without the respirator? She had been here in the hospital now for nearly four weeks. When would she be released and allowed to go home?

As these questions filled her mind, Minerva cried out to God once again for patience and help to accept her circumstances. He heard and showered her burdened heart with His gentle peace. No matter what God asked her to face, she was His servant.

Lovina stood next to the respirator, giving Minerva some breaths by hand with a bag valve mask, or Ambu bag. The mask fit on Minerva's face, with a squeezable bag attached to it. When Lovina squeezed the bag, air flowed to Minerva's lungs.

"Am I going to need this at home?" Minerva asked.

"The doctor said you'll need it wherever you go. We'll probably take it to church, anyway."

After five weeks in the hospital, Minerva was released and allowed to go home. Her family had received a respirator from March of Dimes, and though it didn't have unlimited breathing like the hospital ventilator, she quickly adjusted to it. And just like the doctor had said, the Ambu bag did indeed come in handy. Lovina often pumped air into the tube to give Minerva breaths all the way home from church. Doing it for a length of time, however, got tiring.

"I'll take care of putting Minerva to bed from now on," Lovina told Mom that first night they arrived home from the hospital. As the weeks passed by, Minerva's health continued to improve. The tracheostomy tube in her throat allowed her to whisper, and whenever someone held a finger over the tube's hole, she was able to talk out loud. Life slowly settled back into routine.

One day the medical staff at the hospital received a special letter.

To all those who helped care for me:

I would like to thank each of you for the personal interest you showed in caring for me. I appreciated your concerns.

I have slowly been getting stronger, although a week ago last Saturday I started running a temperature again with quite a bit of pain in my right lung. So I was put back on an antibiotic again, but I am quite a bit better now and am able to be off the machine the equivalent of eight to ten hours a day. I think of you daily and long to see you again.

Affectionately,
Minerva

CHAPTER TWENTY-ONE

Sorrow
1982–1991

Morning sunlight streamed through the bedroom window, forming a warm pool at Minerva's feet as her mother finished braiding her hair. "What are you planning to do today, Mom?" she asked, glancing up.

"I was thinking I would try to get my navy blue dress sewn in time for church tomorrow." Emma set aside the comb and stepped back. "There, that's done. Let's go to the kitchen and have some coffee."

Minerva stood up and followed her mom from the room. On the way through the living room, Emma stopped near the parakeet's cage and opened it. "Come on out, Bobby," she coaxed. The bright blue bird chirped and cocked its head, looking at her curiously. Then he flew toward Minerva and pecked her nose gently. "God bless you," he squawked. "God bless you."

Minerva and her mother laughed as he said the words yet again. "It's like he's kissing you," Emma said, still chuckling as she moved on to the kitchen.

Minerva watched Bobby fondly as he flew away again. They'd had a parakeet once before, but he had died the night she went to the hospital to get her tracheostomy tube. George Norris, who had employed Lovina after she worked for his father Dewitt, heard about the parakeet's death and said he would get Minerva another one. They all liked Bobby.

They took their time sipping the coffee, with Bobby fluttering around them. "I think I'll work in the strawberry patch this afternoon," Emma remarked. "Last night I noticed there are a lot of weeds out there."

Minutes later while Emma arranged two chairs at her sewing machine, Minerva stood at the living room window, watching the road. Occasional vehicles went by, but the summer morning was mostly still. She wondered how Lovina was doing at the bookstore.

When Minerva sat down next to the sewing machine, Mom had already sewn a few seams on her dress. Bobby perched on Mom's head for a while before coming down her temple to her glasses. He peeked around at his reflection in the lenses. "Pretty boy," he chirped softly. "Pretty boy," he said again, flipping his tail.

Minerva shook with laughter as the bird continued his dialogue. "That bird is quite a vain creature!"

"His record gets stuck," Emma said. "He says the same thing over and over again." But she was smiling, and Minerva knew she didn't mind the bird's antics.

That afternoon, Minerva followed her mom to the strawberry patch and sat on the grass to watch as she weeded the rows. She looked at her hands, lying uselessly in her lap, and wished she could help. But she had accepted long ago that this was the way things were.

Glancing upward, she whispered, "Lord, you have given me a good life, and I thank you. I know that this is how I can serve you." Her days were quiet in many respects, but she was content. God had been so good to her, and she simply wanted to bloom where He had placed her.

Trauma touched the Gingerich family in the winter of 1985. Lovina was working at the store when she got a call saying that her brother Noah had died from a heart attack. When she rushed home to be with her family, more of the story unfolded, suggesting another reason for his death.

"Noah knew the bull was in the feedlot this morning," Minerva said. "But the water trough was frozen, so he went into the feedlot to chip away at the ice to make the water available. He had his back turned to the herd, and the bull turned and saw him."

"It seems the bull charged Noah from behind," Mom said, her voice tight with tension. "His body was pushed against the water tank and crushed. His glasses and hat fell off, but he walked out. They traced his footsteps later in the light dusting of snow near the barn, and found that he'd walked a distance before he collapsed. On the road as they went by, people saw him lying there in the lane and slowed down; several stopped to see what they could do. Fannie looked out the window and wondered why these people were stopping. She went out then and tried talking to Noah. She thought he'd had a heart attack and told him she'd get help. He couldn't talk; he just moaned. The squad came out and took him to the hospital, but he was pronounced dead on arrival."

"The doctors at the hospital said that Noah had suffered a heart attack," Minerva said. "They didn't even check out any other possibilities. But when his hat and glasses were found by the water tank, we felt sure the bull had charged him."

It was hard to believe that her brother was gone. Noah had been so outgoing and active, and they had depended on him for many things. Whether it was repairing the basement so water couldn't come in or shoveling snow from their walks, he'd often stopped in to lend a helping hand. But now he was gone, leaving his wife and eleven children behind.

This was the second death in their immediate family. Minerva sat in the nursery using her respirator during the funeral, watching the service through the window. The Gingerich family had grown over the years, and besides nieces and nephews, there were now great-nieces and great-nephews. They rallied around Noah's family, supporting them with their love and prayers, and pointing them to the One who would bear all their burdens and bring healing to their grief.

March winds tugged at Minerva's coat as she walked up to the hospital doors with Fannie and Lovina. "I wonder how Mom is doing," she said, her eyes dark with concern. "She was very sick last night when we left."

"It's hard to believe how fast this happened," Lovina answered softly. They fell silent, thinking back over the events that had brought them to this place.

That week had started out no different than any other. On Tuesday, Lovina had invited some ladies over to help with the quilt she had framed, with plans to sell it at the Haiti Benefit Auction in Holmes County. But by the time the quilters arrived, Emma was experiencing pain in her abdomen. All afternoon while the ladies quilted, she lay in bed.

"Maybe it's the flu," one of the ladies suggested. "It's been going around." But when Emma spent a sleepless night in pain, they took her to the hospital, where tests revealed that scar tissue from a previous surgery had grown around her intestines.

That had been three days before. After the surgery to remove her scar tissue, the doctors had moved her to the ICU. As the sisters now walked down the hall toward the intensive care unit, a nurse stepped out of one of the rooms along the hallway and came toward them.

"Good morning," she called with a smile. Mabel Miller was a Mennonite lady from their community, only a few years older than Lovina, and served as a nurse in the hospital.

"Good morning," Fannie answered, pausing near her. "We're here to visit our mother. She's in the ICU right now."

Mabel glanced down at her chart, and her face sobered. "Do you know how seriously ill your mother is?"

There was silence among the three sisters for a moment. Then Lovina said slowly, "The doctor never told us that she's seriously ill."

"You may visit her one at a time," Mabel said. "But you won't be able to stay very long."

Lovina and Minerva walked on to the waiting room while Fannie went to visit Mom. Minutes later she came into the lobby. Lovina took one look at her face and stood up. "What's wrong?"

"I'm not sure." Fannie's expression was troubled. "Mom keeps picking at her bed covers. One of the nurses said she was doing that all night. I thought maybe she was picking up lint, so I pretended to drop lint on the floor—and then Mom asked, 'Did you throw away my needle?' I don't know what to do! I wish you'd go talk to her, Lovina."

Lovina was already hurrying away. But when she returned, she was chuckling softly. "Mom thought she was quilting," she explained. "I tried to distract her, and she calmed down. But then she asked, 'Did you take my needle?' I said, 'Mom, we're done quilting'—and she answered, 'Oh, good!' But awhile later we went through the same thing again."

"She always has been agreeable," Minerva commented. "She once said that she wants to be like that, so that when she grows old she won't be hard to care for."

"Well, she isn't like Mom on that medication," Fannie said. "But the doctor did say that when older people go through a traumatic experience, they get disoriented. I suppose that's what is happening now."

Mom's health eventually improved and she was able to return home, with no side effects from her surgery. Life settled into its quiet routine once again, filled with cheer and goodwill. Minerva still suffered brief illnesses, and during the winter she was especially vulnerable to colds and pneumonia. But the months turned into years, and God's hand continued to be upon her. Through the loving care of her family and friends, He blessed her richly and filled her heart with a song.

CHAPTER TWENTY-TWO

A Passing

Minerva stood at her mother's bedside, gazing down at her through a mist of tears. At the age of ninety-two, her mother was no longer the strong woman she had once been, able to care for Minerva. Now she was lying in bed as her family cared for her.

The downward process of Emma's health over the past three years had been a slow one as her mind deteriorated. Though she had a walker, she couldn't use it, and she didn't like a cane. "It's dementia, not Alzheimer's," the doctor explained. "If the little blood vessels in the brain burst, they'll break sometimes and cause memory loss." Emma became more restless at night, suffering strokes.

The previous Sunday night, she had taken a turn for the worse. Mom had called to Lovina from her bedroom, and when Lovina went to help her sit up, she fell sideways. "Open and close your hand, Mom," Lovina urged. Mom's response resulted in her hand opening and closing rapidly. Weary from the effort, she complied readily with Lovina's suggestion to sleep again, and Lovina quietly went away.

The next morning, the family received a foreboding message: "Mom had a serious stroke." From near and far they came to be with their mother, knowing that she would not be with them much longer. Finally her left side paralyzed, and she was unable to eat or swallow.

Hearing of their mother's stroke brought fresh grief to the Gingerich family. Only a month earlier, they had laid to rest their brother Ora, who had also suffered a stroke. It seemed too much to bear, but their only choice was to band together and support each other through another sadness.

For five days Mom lay on her deathbed, unable to speak, drink, or swallow. In the evenings the nieces and nephews came to sing, gathering around her bedside. Often she didn't remember their names.

One evening she looked up suddenly at a corner of the wall and pointed. "Eli," she said, the words soft and indistinct with the voice age had given her. "Eli," she repeated, and a holy hush fell over the room. They all knew that Mom's older brother Eli had died a few years ago.

Tears filled many eyes as Mommi kept watching the corner. The end was very near.

Emma Gingerich passed away on January 30, 1999. As they watched the beautiful sunrise clouds through the window, the family felt sure that their mother was resting in the arms of Jesus forever.

Life without Mom seemed empty. She had always been a part of their lives, and now it was only Lovina and Minerva left at home. With Lovina still working at the store, Ida and two other ladies took turns to stay with Minerva on the days Lovina was gone. They brought projects along to work on, and Minerva often read a book. She especially enjoyed the *Budget*, spending hours turning the pages with her lips and reading its contents.

But no matter who was with her, she was always ready to see Lovina return home again.

At times it didn't suit the caretakers to come. On those days Minerva went with Lovina to the store, taking her respirator along. At length she came up with her own solution: she would go with her sister every time, rather than tying someone down to come and stay with her.

By now, Lovina was working only one day a week. The bookstore where she had been working changed hands and became a flea market called "The Corner Cupboard." It was a cute little store filled with shelves of antique items to sell. Lovina also continued to imprint Bibles.

"Around two thousand Bibles have come through here," she said to a customer one morning. "We pray that the many prisoners who received them will surrender their hearts to the Lord."

"Well, it doesn't really matter whose God you worship—Muslim or whatever," answered the lady. "I am a Muslim, and our Koran is what I have grown up with."

Another lady customer joined them. "I was at the library, and I saw your Koran," she said to the Muslim. "I'm a Christian, and I believe in the Bible—but I was inquisitive about the Koran and decided to take it home. When my husband saw it, he told me to take it back to the library. He didn't want it in our house!"

Before the Muslim lady could answer, the door opened. "Good morning!" The Fed-Ex delivery man strode in with a broad smile. "Brought you some more goods to sell. Where shall I put these boxes?"

"Put them back here behind the counter," Lovina said. "We'll take care of it later." She turned back to the discussion at hand. "I don't agree with your idea that it doesn't matter whose God we worship," she said kindly to the Muslim lady. "We must worship the Lord only."

"Are you a Muslim?" The Fed-Ex driver straightened and turned toward the lady. At her nod, he exclaimed, "So am I! I brought my wife and children over to America, but she didn't like it here and went back. I stay here and send her money now." He glanced at Lovina. "I would like to marry again—Muslims are allowed to have five wives. But I don't want a lady who wears shorts. I want someone who wears skirts, so I guess I'll have to get one of your Mennonite girls."

Minerva grinned and shook her head. "They won't marry you!"

"That isn't right, sir," Lovina added more soberly. "Have you read our Bible?"

He nodded. "I've read it through."

"You have to serve the living God—our God," Lovina said.

"If I disagree with you, will you get mad?" the Fed-Ex driver asked.

"No," answered Lovina. "But if I don't agree with you, will you get mad?" As she spoke, she handed a receipt to a lady whose items she had just checked out.

"I won't," he answered. "But I would like to ask some more questions." He turned to Minerva. "Do you celebrate Christmas?"

"Oh, yes. Do you?"

He shook his head. "No. We don't believe in Jesus; the Saviour hasn't come yet."

"Yes, He has," Minerva answered simply.

He smiled a little. "Well, I can see we aren't going to agree about these things. I wish you would read our Koran. Now don't say no!" he added as Minerva shook her head. "I'll bring it sometime so you can read it."

"I won't read it, sir," she answered respectfully. "I believe in the one true God."

When the Fed-Ex driver finally left the store, Minerva and Lovina smiled at each other. "We get into quite the discussions, don't we?" Lovina asked, turning toward the door as it opened again. "Why, it's Jim and Darlene! Hello," she called to them. "Isn't it a beautiful day that God has made?"

"Yes," answered Darlene with a smile, glancing in her direction. She went on down the aisle while Jim came over to them, ready as usual to talk about the Lord and the Bible. After a lengthy conversation, he smiled as his wife came to the counter with her items. "I always come in and preach to you, don't I?" he asked good-naturedly.

Lovina and Minerva looked at each other and laughed. These customers were their friends, and they kept the days interesting.

CHAPTER TWENTY-THREE

Surgery
September 2, 2010

"My stomach hurts, Lovina." Minerva turned slowly in her chair, grimacing with pain.

Lovina looked at her with concern. Her sister hadn't slept well the night before. Maybe this stomachache was the reason.

"Come with me to the kitchen," she said. "I'll give you some Pepto-Bismol."

Though she was doubtful of how much the medicine would help, Minerva followed her sister to the kitchen. Minutes later she paused at the window and looked out. The day was overcast, filling their little house with shadows. Vehicles rushed by on the road, slowing to let one car pull into their driveway. "Someone is coming," she called.

Lovina came to her side, her eyes lighting up when she saw the vehicle. "Why, it's David!" Their nephew hailed from Linneus, Missouri. Hurrying to the door, she opened it wide. "Come in, come in!"

David stepped inside, smiling. "I just came into the area last night. I thought I'd come and visit you this morning."

"We're so glad you did." Lovina closed the door and gestured toward the living room. "Come on in and sit down! Would you like a cup of coffee?"

"Thanks, but I already had some." David leaned back in his chair. "I was wondering if the two of you would like to go with me to Belle Center today. I'm not too sure how to get there anyway, and I thought you might welcome the chance to go up there."

"It does sound like a good opportunity," Lovina said slowly. "Do you think you're up to going along, Minerva?"

Minerva hesitated, but then she nodded. "I'll try to. But I need to take my respirator along, or I'll get too tired."

"Sure, we can take your respirator," David said cheerfully. "How have you been doing these days?"

"I didn't feel very good when I woke up this morning," Minerva admitted. "But Lovina gave me some Pepto-Bismol, so I'm hoping I'll feel better soon."

Concern swept across David's face. "If you'd rather not go today—"

Minerva shook her head. "I'm sure it'll be fine. And I want to go with you! I don't often get to see Dan's and Verna's families since they moved away."

"Well, if you're sure," David said hesitantly. He glanced at his watch. "I thought we could leave in a half hour or so."

"We'll be ready when you are," Minerva assured him.

The day seemed to fly, and twilight was falling by the time they arrived home from Belle Center at 6:00 that evening. David carried the respirator into the house and then left to spend the night with his brother Wayne's family.

That night for their devotions, Lovina read a verse from Psalms. "The lines are fallen unto me in pleasant places; yea, I have a goodly heritage." She glanced up. "We had an enjoyable time today with our relatives, didn't we?"

"It was a very good time together," Minerva answered softly.

"Now that Mom is gone, I treasure every moment I can spend with my family. Time seems fleeting, especially when I think of how fragile my own health is."

Lovina glanced at her pale face, and alarm touched her heart. But she waited until bedtime to ask Minerva about it. "Is your pain from this morning better by now?"

"No. If anything, it's worse."

Lovina's hands trembled slightly as she covered her sister's frail form with the blanket. "Well, try to sleep now, and maybe you'll feel better by morning."

But Minerva's pain was so severe by morning that they both knew something had to be done. Lovina called Ida, who agreed to take Minerva to the emergency room immediately. There she was given an orange liquid called "contrast" to drink, so the doctors could perform a CT scan to better determine the cause of her pain. The drink would accentuate her gastrointestinal tract on the scan, allowing the doctors to find any problems more easily.

"Well, I have good news and bad news," surgeon Dr. Fisher said when he came out to the room where the three sisters were waiting. "The good news is that we know the problem is with Minerva's appendix. The bad news is that she'll need surgery." He glanced at his chart and turned to Minerva. "I think we'll schedule your surgery for 2:00, or maybe 3:00; some other surgeries are scheduled before then."

It wasn't until 4:30 that Minerva was taken into surgery. With the doctor's promise to meet them in the lobby on the first floor after the surgery was over, Lovina and Ida sat down to wait. Time seemed to drag by, and they were both intensely relieved when Dr. Fisher finally came out.

"The laparoscopic surgery took longer than I expected," he told them. "Minerva's appendix had already ruptured, and there was pus, bile, and even stool in the abdominal cavity. I irrigated it thoroughly, as I didn't want to do any more cutting. She's a very sick girl. She's in the ICU now, and you can go up to see her if you like."

When the sisters entered the ICU, they found Minerva sleeping. She had been hooked up to a respirator and IV, with a tube in her nose and abdomen. Lovina and Ida stood looking down at her pale, sickly form. They wondered if she would make it through this alive.

"Is this your sister?" Dr. Jessica Goeller had come into the room and was standing beside them, her soft eyes watching them closely. At Lovina's nod, she went on, "I was Minerva's anesthesiologist during the surgery. I changed her trach to a non-fenestrated cuffed trach so no fluids could get into her lungs. When they laid her down for surgery, the contrast drink she had before the surgery would have come up and suffocated her."

As Dr. Goeller moved on, Lovina and Ida looked at each other, too moved to speak. They knew that this woman had helped to save their sister's life.

The non-fenestrated tracheostomy tube that Dr. Goeller had given Minerva took away her ability to talk out loud or even whisper. When visitors came on Sunday afternoon, she was too ill to make much response.

But as evening fell, Minerva became restless. "Get me out of here," she mouthed to Lovina.

"You're too sick to get up," Lovina answered, moving closer to the bed.

"Well, sit me up!" Minerva struggled upward, her face pale with the effort.

Quickly placing her hands on Minerva's shoulders, Lovina pushed her back. "You can't get up, Minnie. Just lie still, okay?"

"What's wrong?" A nurse stepped into the room.

Minerva tried to explain. "It doesn't feel like my respirator is giving me the air I need." She was thankful that Lovina could understand the silent words and convey this message to the nurse.

"We'll put you on some medication," the nurse decided. "The Ativan will help you rest better."

When Verna and her twin daughters Miriam and Martha arrived from Belle Center that evening, Minerva was indeed feeling better and could welcome them with joy. "We want to stay here in the hospital with you for the night," Martha told her. She had so many memories of this special aunt. It hurt to see Minerva struggling through yet another hospital stay.

On September 8, Minerva was moved out of the ICU. They all liked the new, spacious room, with its windows that let in the bright sunlight. "You may stay in her room all day if you wish," one of the nurses told Lovina and Ida. This was a relief to them all.

Ida's daughter Lisa, a licensed massage therapist, came in to help with Minerva's care. She massaged her aunt's back and feet, and she changed damp pillows and towels. Though the nurses tried to keep Minerva in an upright position with pillows propped behind her, her body kept sliding down. So in addition to pulling her up and rearranging her often, the sisters also needed to change Minerva's gown because of the fluids that kept leaking from her drain tubes. "I think I kept the girls busy," Minerva dictated in a letter to a friend, adding a smiley face behind it. But she was thankful that they could be close by at all times.

On September 10, one week after she had been admitted to

the hospital, the doctors put Minerva on a liquid diet of chicken broth, juice, and jello. Visitors came in a steady stream, with nurses coming and going. Through it all Minerva remained in a sedated condition, sleepy and unable to give her visitors the attention she would have liked.

But gradually she began to improve, gaining strength with each day. This was not without its snags, however. *After lunch today, Minerva was sitting on the bedside and couldn't get her breath,* Lovina wrote in her journal one day. *She turned ashen, her lips turned blue, and she felt faint. The emergency personnel were called and they rushed into Minerva's room, where they gave her some breaths with the resuscitator bag. Minerva revived again, and slept connected to her PLV100 respirator all night.*

The day that Minerva was discharged was a happy one for all of them. *Dr. Fisher and Dr. Skytta came in and discharged her,* Lovina recorded in her journal. *We left by 4:45, and all went well on the way home. After we got settled in at home, Dan's and Abe's families came from Belle Center. Soon Minerva couldn't get enough air again, and started to faint. Mark Kemmerer, her respiratory therapist, came and tried to readjust the respirator, but she still felt faint. Mark went home then, and Dan and Abe went home with their families too, leaving Verna here to help. When we resuscitated Minerva, she got more air and didn't feel quite as faint, but when we put her back on her PLV100 respirator, she felt faint again. It was bedtime, so we decided to put her to bed with a PVV respirator, which she sleeps with. That one gave her sufficient air.*

Day by day Minerva grew stronger. Eventually she was able to go to church and enjoy normal activities again. But the laparoscopic surgery had taken something out of her. Before her appendix burst, Minerva had been able to stay off the respirator all day, but after that she needed to get on it by noon. Without the air pumping into her body, she would have been too tired to survive.

Mark Kemmerer came to check her respirator every three months to make sure everything was working properly. It regularly needed to be replaced with a serviced one. Minerva had two respirators at all times in case one stopped working, which didn't happen often.

"I brought you a pineapple cake with cream cheese icing," Mark said one day when he arrived. "It's something I made myself."

"Really?" Lovina took the cake and sliced two pieces for herself and Minerva. "This is so kind of you!"

"You'll have to give us the recipe," Minerva declared after one bite.

Mark grinned. "I'll give it to you as soon as I check out your respirator."

Minerva came closer to watch him work, thankful for God's continued protection and healing. This experience had strengthened her faith, renewing her resolve to bloom where she was planted and serve the Lord as long as she lived.

CHAPTER TWENTY-FOUR

Celebrations
2011–2014

Changes came to their lives as the seasons marched on. Over the years the Amish people moved away, died, or joined the Amish Mennonite (Beachy) churches in the community, eventually leaving only five elderly ladies in the Amish church. Ministers from Holmes County, Ohio, took turns preaching for them every two weeks until the church house was sold. Finally they began attending Bethesda Amish Mennonite Church several miles away. They attended services every Sunday, except for communion. On those days they traveled up to Belle Center, where Dan and Verna were living with their families.

People from Bethesda often stopped in to visit. One evening Lovina answered the knock on the door and found Ray and Bertie Stutzman standing on the steps. "Come in, come in! It's good to see you!"

"We thought we'd stop in for a while tonight," Bertie said as she stepped inside.

They shook hands, and Lovina motioned toward the living room. "Take a seat—any you like!"

Bertie stopped next to Minerva, touching her shoulder. "How are you, Minerva?"

Minerva, sitting at a small card table with the *Budget* spread out before her, smiled up at her. "Good!" She had gone to school with both Bertie and Ray, and thus had known them for years.

"Have you read that whole thing?" Ray asked with a grin.

Minerva's dark eyes crinkled with laughter. No matter what Ray asked her about *Budget* news, she always knew what he was talking about. "I just finished reading the back cover."

They discussed community news and talked about their own lives. "It's not that I don't wonder sometimes how things would be without my polio," Minerva remarked. "But I have so much to be thankful for."

Her friends smiled. Minerva's cheerful outlook on life was always such a blessing.

Twilight was falling by the time Ray mentioned that he had brought along his harmonica. "Shall I play a song or two before we leave?" he asked.

"Oh, yes, yes!" Minerva nodded vigorously. A smile touched her lips as Ray played the song "There's a City of Light." What a privilege it was to have friends. They touched her life in so many ways.

———

Lovina and Minerva still worked at the store once a week on Mondays. Each time, they prayed that they would be a witness for God. Many customers came over from another part of the store "just to see if they were there." From her chair behind the counter, Minerva would stand up and call, "Hello!"

"I haven't seen you in a long time, Minerva," a lady said one morning, returning her greeting. "Give me a hug—I gotta have a hug!"

Minerva was watching her walk away when the doorbell jangled again, signaling the arrival of another customer. Minerva turned and saw a young girl coming toward her. She had no idea who the girl was, but she smiled and called once again. "Hello!"

"Hi!" The girl came toward her, a smile sparkling in her eyes. "I want to pray for you," she said without preamble. Reaching out to hold Minerva's arms, the girl prayed aloud, asking God to bless Minerva and give her strength.

Later that day, Minerva shared the story with a customer who came in. "That was my daughter," the lady said with a smile. "She heard how you were stricken with polio and paralyzed from it."

"That was a long time ago," Minerva mused. Nearly sixty years had passed since she'd first been in the hospital with polio. She was seventy-three years old now, and Lovina was nearly eighty. How fast the years had flown. They had shared a lot together. "You never see one without the other," a sister at Bethesda had remarked. That was definitely true. Minerva didn't know what she'd do without Lovina. Through her, God provided companionship and someone to be her hands. They were very close.

"What are we doing here?" Lovina looked around in bewilderment at all the vehicles in the Haven church parking lot.

From where she was walking beside her, Ida smiled. "Never mind; just go on in."

Minerva was curious too. "They probably forgot about my birthday," Lovina had told her. Certainly no one had said anything about it until Corny and Ida offered to take them out to eat for supper. When they'd turned into the parking lot at Haven, Lovina's suspicions were immediately aroused.

Now as they walked through the doors, Lovina gasped and stopped short. Minerva stepped around her, staring in amazement at the many tables set up in the fellowship hall. People were everywhere—her siblings, nieces and nephews, and friends—all smiling and singing "Happy Birthday."

Beside Minerva, Lovina swallowed hard, not sure whether to laugh or cry. They were coming toward her now, surrounding her with laughter and well-wishes for her eightieth birthday. There was her sister Verna from Belle Center, who'd evaded Lovina's earlier suggestion of coming to see Lester and Sarah. "They're here for a ministers' meeting," Lovina had told her. "I thought you might want to come and see them."

"I don't know if it's going to work out or not," Verna answered. "We're having communion on Sunday." But now she was here, and Lovina couldn't help but laugh. What a surprise this was.

Even her former employer George Norris and his wife Linda were there. They sat next to Lovina and Minerva at the dinner table, a privilege for them all. "Go right ahead and visit with your family, Lovina," said George when she pushed back her empty plate. "I'll finish feeding Minerva for you."

"Thank you," she smiled, standing up. As she wove through the crowd, tears pressed against her eyes again. *I have a full life with my family,* she had told Mom and Minerva once. Those words echoed in her heart today, filling it with peace. She was richly blessed.

July 1, 2012, was another celebration of life. This time Ida had placed an ad in the *Budget,* inviting friends and family to an open house at Haven Fellowship Church to observe the sixtieth anniversary of when Minerva was first stricken with polio. In addition to family, all the Mennonite churches in the Plain City community were well-represented.

Minerva stood with Lovina at her side, greeting the people

who filed through to meet her. "It can't be," she murmured in disbelief, looking out over the crowd. "This many people!"

"Minerva!" An elderly lady had stopped near her, leaning on her cane, her face wreathed in smiles. "I was so tickled when I saw that ad in the paper. I knew I had to come!" She placed a wrinkled hand on Minerva's arm. "My husband was one of your doctors when you first went to the hospital. Perhaps you remember him—Dr. Frank Lyons?"

"Dr. Lyons!" Minerva's face lit up. "He was one of my special doctors."

The lady's eyes were soft. "He always spoke highly of the girl with polio who was a brave fighter and wanted to live."

As she walked on, Minerva gazed after her. Mrs. Lyons' words brought back memories of long ago—memories of the time that had shaped the course of her life. So much had happened; so much had changed. Where would she be today without the sustaining grace of her Lord?

When at last everyone was through, four hundred names had been signed in the guest book. Someone had set out a little basket for people to put in encouraging cards, and quite a few gave money along with the cards. Minerva felt humbled as she watched the people go through the food line, where an abundance of cookies, snacks, and coffee had been set out. *Why me? Who am I to be noticed in this way?* She knew it was only by the Lord's grace that she had made it this far. God had a special plan for her life, and she wanted to do all she could to be worthy of it.

Minerva sat in her usual place behind the counter at the store, watching Lovina as she checked out customers one by one.

Occasionally some came to talk with her, while others merely smiled and walked on.

Then she heard the familiar question: "What is that thing for?"

"You mean my respirator?" Minerva followed the lady's gaze. "My lungs are weak, and I need it to breathe."

"Why?" The lady stepped closer, her gaze open and curious.

"I had polio," Minerva said simply.

"Oh my," the lady breathed. Reaching out, she placed her hands on Minerva's shoulders. "God has a purpose for you yet. Keep on being a light." She paused, then asked, "Can you use your hands?" When Minerva shook her head, the lady took Minerva's hand in her own. Closing her eyes, she prayed aloud, "Oh, Lord, give her strength!"

Drawing back again, she gazed into Minerva's face. "How old are you?"

"I'm seventy-five," answered Minerva, smiling.

"You don't look that old!" She chuckled, and Minerva laughed too.

"I can't use my arms and hands, but they don't ache," she said.

They chatted a few minutes longer before the lady revealed her identity. "I am the chaplain of the Women's Correctional Institute in Springfield, Ohio."

When she left, Minerva turned to Lovina. "You know, I would hate to quit working here," she said thoughtfully. "Everyone is so kind to us."

Lovina smiled. "We've made a lot of friends."

"I feel that with my handicap, I can reach the most people for God this way," Minerva went on, her voice softer now. "I want to be a testimony for God, and not be discontent. Lots of people are worse off than I am."

The sound of wheels crunching on gravel outside broke into their conversation. "It looks like another customer just arrived," said Lovina, glancing out the window. "Oh, it's Betty, the lady who has a ministry of sending cards to people." She smiled. "I wonder if she'll buy six boxes again today."

Minerva smiled too. "Our prayer is always to be a witness, but it seems that our customers are witnesses too."

"Yes," agreed Lovina, her voice soft. "We are blessed—so blessed. God is good to us."

Afterword

May 30, 2014 · Plain City, Ohio

The day I attend the Gingerich reunion is sunny and warm. I sit with Minerva and Lovina inside where it's cool, observing their family as they gather around them. I feel as though I'm a part of this gathering, yet I know I'm here only because of a story I'm writing. But the story intertwines my heart with theirs irrevocably, and I know that I will leave this place with new friends.

As the afternoon wanes, the family gathers to sing. One tradition at a Gingerich reunion is that the siblings get up to sing for the others, but this year only six are here—Minerva, Lovina, Verna, Ida, Lester, and Dan. As they sing, I can hear echoes of how it used to be years ago. They are aging now, and time has brought changes to their family. Three brothers have already passed on, and one sister is unable to be here because of an illness.

We all sing the final song together, a hymn that made an impression on the young Minerva so many years ago: "No Tears in Heaven." As the melody flows around me, I watch Minerva and can't help but think how much God must be looking forward to calling her home. I can almost see her standing inside the shining gates of heaven, the light of the Son surrounding her with a radiant glow, her body made complete and whole. A lump comes into my throat as I look back down at my songbook.

> *"Some morning yonder, we'll cease to ponder*
> *O'er things this life has brought to view;*
> *All will be clearer, loved ones be dearer,*
> *In heav'n where all will be made new . . ."*
>
> —Diane Yoder

A Note from the Author

When I first came to Plain City, Ohio, to interview Minerva Gingerich for her story, I knew she had polio as a young girl and had been paralyzed from the disease. Beyond that I knew almost nothing.

As I spent time with Minerva, listening to her tell her story with each breath the respirator allowed her to take, I marveled at this lady's courage and strength. "It was always an accepted fact that I was paralyzed," she told me. "I don't recall ever struggling with it; I just felt that this was the way I would live my life, and it was how the Lord wanted me to be a witness for Him."

A witness for Him. The words struck me deeply as she went on. "I want to accept my handicap and just bloom where I'm planted. Because God knows all about us and has helped me through the trying times, I want to do whatever He asks of me and be happy. He did so much more for me. We had no idea that He would preserve my life this long."

Minerva is truly a witness for Christ in her cheerfulness and uncomplaining acceptance of her circumstances. Lovina shines in her patient care for Minerva; she is her younger sister's hands. The two are very close, and God works through them to touch many lives. I hope their story has blessed you as it blessed me.

About the Author

Diane Yoder hones her story-writing craft in southern Indiana, where she lives with her parents and three of her siblings. A longtime lover of writing, Diane published her first story when she was fourteen years old. Through the encouragement of her friends and family, she decided to pursue her dream of writing books. She has written *Betteken's Refuge* (published by TGS) and *Where the Road Divides* and *Pardon's Price* (published by Ridgeway). All three of these books are available through TGS.

Diane is a member of Living Waters Mennonite Church. She delights in the beauty she finds in nature, music, words, and people. Her desire and prayer is that her readers will learn to trust the Saviour and receive His love.

If you wish to contact Diane, you may write to her at 10279 West Polk Road, Lexington, IN 47138, or at Christian Aid Ministries, P.O. Box 360, Berlin, Ohio 44610. She would be happy to hear from you!

About the Gingeriches

Minerva and Lovina Gingerich would also welcome letters from readers. If you wish to contact them, you may write to them at 15176 State Route 161 W, Plain City, Ohio 43064.

Christian Aid Ministries

Christian Aid Ministries was founded in 1981 as a nonprofit, tax-exempt 501(c)(3) organization. Its primary purpose is to provide a trustworthy and efficient channel for Amish, Mennonite, and other conservative Anabaptist groups and individuals to minister to physical and spiritual needs around the world. This is in response to the command ". . . do good unto all men, especially unto them who are of the household of faith" (Galatians 6:10).

Each year, CAM supporters provide approximately 15 million pounds of food, clothing, medicines, seeds, Bibles, Bible story books, and other Christian literature for needy people. Most of the aid goes to orphans and Christian families. Supporters' funds also help to clean up and rebuild for natural disaster victims, put up Gospel billboards in the U.S., support several church-planting efforts, operate two medical clinics, and provide resources for needy families to make their own living. CAM's main purposes for providing aid are to help and encourage God's people and bring the Gospel to a lost and dying world.

CAM has staff, warehouses, and distribution networks in Romania, Moldova, Ukraine, Haiti, Nicaragua, Liberia, and Israel. Aside from management, supervisory personnel, and bookkeeping operations, volunteers do most of the work at CAM locations. Each year, volunteers at our warehouses, field bases, Disaster Response Services projects, and other locations donate over 200,000 hours of work.

CAM's ultimate purpose is to glorify God and help enlarge His kingdom. ". . . whatsoever ye do, do all to the glory of God" (1 Corinthians 10:31).

The Way to God and Peace

We live in a world contaminated by sin. Sin is anything that goes against God's holy standards. When we do not follow the guidelines that God our Creator gave us, we are guilty of sin. Sin separates us from God, the source of life.

Since the time when the first man and woman, Adam and Eve, sinned in the Garden of Eden, sin has been universal. The Bible says that we all have "sinned and come short of the glory of God" (Romans 3:23). It also says that the natural consequence for that sin is eternal death, or punishment in an eternal hell: "Then when lust hath conceived, it bringeth forth sin: and sin, when it is finished, bringeth forth death" (James 1:15).

But we do not have to suffer eternal death in hell. God provided forgiveness for our sins through the death of His only Son, Jesus Christ. Because Jesus was perfect and without sin, He could die in our place. "For God so loved the world that he gave his only begotten Son, that whosoever believeth in him should not perish, but have everlasting life" (John 3:16).

A sacrifice is something given to benefit someone else. It costs the giver greatly. Jesus was God's sacrifice. Jesus' death takes away the penalty of sin for everyone who accepts this sacrifice and truly repents of their sins. To repent of sins means to be truly sorry for and turn away from the things we have done that have violated God's standards (Acts 2:38; 3:19).

Jesus died, but He did not remain dead. After three days, God's Spirit miraculously raised Him to life again. God's Spirit does something similar in us. When we receive Jesus as our sacrifice and repent of our sins, our hearts are changed. We become spiritually alive! We develop new desires and attitudes

(2 Corinthians 5:17). We begin to make choices that please God (1 John 3:9). If we do fail and commit sins, we can ask God for forgiveness. "If we confess our sins, he is faithful and just to forgive us our sins, and to cleanse us from all unrighteousness" (1 John 1:9).

Once our hearts have been changed, we want to continue growing spiritually. We will be happy to let Jesus be the Master of our lives and will want to become more like Him. To do this, we must meditate on God's Word and commune with God in prayer. We will testify to others of this change by being baptized and sharing the good news of God's victory over sin and death. Fellowship with a faithful group of believers will strengthen our walk with God (1 John 1:7).